Translation Theories

CW00521864

Translation Theories Explained is a series designed to respond to the profound plurality of contemporary translation studies. There are many problems to be solved, many possible approaches that can be drawn from neighbouring disciplines, and several strong language-bound traditions plagued by the paradoxical fact that some of the key theoretical texts have yet to be translated.

Recognizing this plurality as both a strength and a potential shortcoming, the series provides a format where different approaches can be compared, their virtues assessed, and mutual blind spots overcome. There will also be scope for introductions to specific areas of translation practice. Students and scholars may thus gain comprehensive awareness of the work being done beyond local or endemic frames.

Most volumes in the series place a general approach within its historical context, giving examples to illustrate the main ideas, summarizing the most significant debates and opening perspectives for future work. The authors have been selected not only because of their command of a particular approach but also in view of their openness to alternatives and their willingness to discuss criticisms. In every respect the emphasis is on explaining the essential points as clearly and as concisely as possible, using numerous examples and providing glossaries of the main technical terms.

The series should prove particularly useful to students dealing with translation theories for the first time, to teachers seeking to stimulate critical reflection, and to scholars looking for a succinct overview of the field's present and future.

Anthony Pym
Series Editor

Can Theory Help Translators?

A dialogue between the ivory tower and the wordface

Andrew Chesterman and Emma Wagner

Routledge
Taylor & Francis Group

LONDON AND NEW YORK

First published 2002 by St. Jerome Publishing
Second edition published 2010

Published 2014 by Routledge
2 Park Square, Milton Park, Abingdon, Oxon OX14 4RN
711 Third Avenue, New York, NY 10017, USA

Routledge is an imprint of the Taylor & Francis Group, an informa business

Notices
Knowledge and best practice in this field are constantly changing. As new research and experience broaden our understanding, changes in research methods, professional practices, or medical treatment may become necessary.

Practitioners and researchers must always rely on their own experience and knowledge in evaluating and using any information, methods, compounds, or experiments described herein. In using such information or methods they should be mindful of their own safety and the safety of others, including parties for whom they have a professional responsibility.

To the fullest extent of the law, neither the Publisher nor the authors, contributors, or editors, assume any liability for any injury and/or damage to persons or property as a matter of products liability, negligence or otherwise, or from any use or operation of any methods, products, instructions, or ideas contained in the material herein.

ISBN 13: 978-1-900650-49-6 (pbk)
ISSN 1365-0513 (*Translation Theories Explained*)

Cover design by
Steve Fieldhouse, Oldham, UK

Typeset by
Delta Typesetters, Cairo, Egypt

British Library Cataloguing in Publication Data
A catalogue record of this book is available from the British Library

Library of Congress Cataloging-in-Publication Data
Chesterman, Andrew.
  Can theory help translators? : a dialogue between the ivory tower and the wordface /
Andrew Chesterman and Emma Wagner.
      p. cm. -- (Translation theories explained, ISSN ISSN 1365-0513)
  Includes bibliographical references and index.
  ISBN 1-900650-49-5 (alk. paper)
  1. Translating and interpreting. I. Wagner, Emma. II. Title. III. Series.
  P306 .C534 2001
  418'.02--dc21

                          2001001852

Contents

Preface

This book started as a critical response by Emma Wagner to Andrew Chesterman's book *Memes of Translation: The spread of ideas in translation theory* (1997). Interesting stuff, she said, but not really the book that will convince practising translators that there is anything in translation theory that might be of use to them. We began a correspondence by e-mail, and the discussion touched on many aspects of translation theory and practice. It soon occurred to us that the exchange might be worth developing and publishing as a book, for others to join in. We sketched a plan for themes we wanted to discuss, and continued our correspondence. The book preserves this dialogue form, and the editing has been minimal. The style thus remains rather informal; bibliographical references in the text were added later.

The main issue is the relation between translation theory and translation practice. The theory seeks to describe and explain the practice, yes; but practitioners seem also to look to the theory for guidance. What do they find there?

We discuss many themes that are important to both theory and practice: the translator's identity and changing historical role, the translator's visibility, translation types and strategies, professional translation quality, ethics, and translation aids.

Emma Wagner (EW) is a translator and translation manager at the European Commission in Luxembourg. She is the initiator of the Fight the FOG campaign to encourage clear writing at the European Commission. Andrew Chesterman (AC) is currently professor of translation theory at the University of Helsinki, Finland.

We would like to thank several friends and colleagues for their comments on earlier versions of the manuscript: Brian McCluskey and Dave Skinner in Brussels; Poul Andersen in Luxembourg; David Harris in London; and Ritva Leppihalme and Diana Tullberg in Helsinki. We also thank Bill Fraser and Helen Titchen, English translators at the European Commission, for permission to include their material on 'distancing' in Chapter 5. Our thanks also to St. Jerome Publishing and their editor Anthony Pym for encouraging us.

Emma Wagner wishes to point out that the views expressed here are her own and not those of the European Commission; but her own views have been formed by contact with many other translators – some of whom are quoted directly, some indirectly – and she would like to thank them all, named and nameless.

November 2000   EW, Luxembourg   AC, Helsinki

1. Is translation theory relevant to translators' problems?

EW

'Translation theory? Spare us...' That's the reaction to be expected from most practising translators. Messages from the ivory tower tend not to penetrate as far as the wordface. (The wordface is the place where we translators work – think of a miner at the coalface.)

Most of us had a brief brush with theory in our student days, when we absorbed whatever was needed to get us through our exams... and then proceeded to forget it, as we got to grips with the realities of learning how to do the job. There can be few professions with such a yawning gap between theory and practice.

About a decade ago Lars Berglund (1990:148), a technical translator in Germany, wrote a damning article about the irrelevance of translation studies:

> With the current approach, translation studies of the kind pursued at West German universities produce few results of interest to people outside the community formed by the translation scholars themselves. ... We need more orientation toward the needs and interests of practising translators and their clients.

Has anything changed? Have translation theorists produced anything of relevance for practising translators or their clients?

Recently Graham Cross (1998:27), a British translator, reviewed the Routledge *Encyclopedia of Translation Studies*, concluding that it was

> a remarkable storehouse of interesting information. But my doubts about the book's aims remain. Will it help one to become a better translator? I doubt it. ... Does it help to give the translation profession a feeling of self-esteem and worth? Hardly. ... From the point of view of my working life, it is interesting but irrelevant.

So tell me, how wrong are we? What's translation theory about? Can it help us to become better translators and give us a feeling of professional self-esteem?

AC

Your opening move raises some big issues. I'll start with your last point and work backwards.

Can translation theory help translators? In a way, I have a lot of sympathy with what I suppose is the assumption behind this question: that's one reason why we are writing this book, after all. But let's ponder the assumption a bit first: that translation theory SHOULD have this aim.

Would you pose the same question of other kinds of theory, I wonder? Should musicology help musicians or composers to become better musicians or composers? Should literary theory help writers and poets to write better? Should sociology help the people and groups it studies to become better members of society? Should the theories of mechanics and cybernetics help engineers and computer scientists to produce better robots? I guess your answers to these questions will not be identical: I myself would be more inclined to answer yes to the last one than to the others. To the sociology one, I might answer that it should at least help people like politicians to make better decisions. But the ones on musicology and literary theory seem a bit different; such theories seem more to help other people understand these art forms, rather than the artists themselves. In particular, such theories might help academics (theorists) to understand something better, and hence, in some abstract way, add to the sum total of cultural knowledge.

So is translation theory more like musicology and literary theory, or like sociology, or like mechanics and cybernetics? From the point of view of a practising translator, it may seem more like the mechanics type.

As such its value (its only value?) is in its application, in its social usefulness. This connects with your initial coal-mining metaphor (to which I shall return later!). We are mining coal, so let's have a theory that makes the job easier, helps us to mine more efficiently...

On this view, theorists are somehow seen to be 'up there', like teachers, in possession of knowledge to hand down, or at least with the duty of finding out such information; and we translators are 'down here' (underground?): just tell us what to do, tell us how to do it better, please... What kind of a professional self-image emerges here?

Most modern translation theorists find this view very odd. To them, it seems to represent an old-fashioned prescriptive approach, an approach that sets out to state what people should do. For several decades now, mainstream translation theory has tried to get away from this approach: it has been thought unscientific, un-empirical. Instead, we theorists should seek to be descriptive, to describe, explain and understand what translators do actually do, not stipulate what they ought to do. From this descriptive point of view, it is the translators that are 'up there', performing an incredibly complex activity, and the theorists are 'down here', trying to understand how on earth the translators manage. These theorists see themselves as studying the translators, not instructing them.

Having said this, I do think that lots of bits of translation theory are nevertheless relevant to translators... But let's see, as this dialogue progresses.

I wonder if we can agree on what the aims of a translation theory ought to be? And on what the research object of such a theory might be, what we would expect it to cover? The word 'theory' originally meant a way of seeing, a perspective from which to contemplate something, so as to understand.

So a lot depends on your point of view, on your theory of what a translation theory should be.

As a way of opening this topic, I invite you to imagine that someone has just invented a new academic discipline, known as Chair Theory. This purports to be a complete theory of the chair. (Chairs are man-made objects, like translations...) What would you imagine Chair Theory to cover, what would its aims be, what would its various subsections be?

EW

If Chair Theory existed, I think it should:

a) observe: find out about all the types of chair that exist; study chairs through the ages, chairs around the world;
b) analyze: distil a few generalizations out of all the observation:
* definition of chair and main categories of chair;
* constraints of chair design (human anatomy; intended function – dining chair, office chair, deck chair, etc.);
* constraints of chair production (materials available, manufacturing methods, etc);
c) guide: set out the underlying principles and doctrines of the craft.

Its purpose should be to help the producers and users of chairs by:

* saving them all the work of observing and analyzing for themselves;
* coining a common language for use by chair makers, chair users and chair theorists;
* setting tentative standards, providing some guidance as to what can reasonably be expected of a chair, depending on the intended function.

Only when they have done all this should chair theorists be allowed to indulge in cogitation about Plato's Ideal Chair and the 'chair *an sich*', and to ask difficult questions like 'Are chairs possible?', 'Is a chair still a chair, even when there's no one sitting there?', etc. Above all they should resist the urge to base their theories on the few chairs they happen to have sat on (or made!) themselves, or seen dotted around the university canteen.

Replace the word 'chair' by 'translation' and you can see what I think translation theory should be about. Roughly.

So you say that for the past few decades translation theory has been getting away from a prescriptive approach and has tried to describe, explain and understand what translators do actually do. Sounds interesting! But in the past two and a half decades I've spent working in the largest translation service in the world, there have been very few sightings of translation theorists of any stripe – prescriptive, descriptive or otherwise. Nor have our products or problems been deemed worthy of study. Translations of *Alice in Wonderland* are obviously so much more interesting than the multilingual legislation, reports and correspondence that we churn out on an industrial scale to fuel international cooperation.

AC

Chair theory might also be interested in such themes as chairs and power (thrones...), chairs and communication (seating arrangements...), carpenters' decision-making processes, the relation between chairs and other furniture, how chairs age, when they become outdated and need replacing...

Translation theory has been interested in corresponding matters, and has in fact dealt with all your required topics. It has done a lot of observing – your category (a) – although most of this work has been on literary translation, true. This focus has been partly for practical reasons: there are lots of literary translations to observe, especially if you also happen to be interested in cultural history, and a lot of this translation-theoretical work has been in the tradition of comparative literature and cultural studies. Literary translation has traditionally had a high status, after all: such texts are seen as Culturally Important.

But in recent years there have also been many publications on technical translation, scientific translation, and what some people call 'pragmatic translation' – i.e. looking at non-literary texts (such as those you deal with). Some of this research comes out of text linguistics and genre studies. Typical topics might be: characteristic problems in translating machine operation instructions, tourist brochures, legislative texts, recipes, academic abstracts, etc.

Your categories (b) and (c) have also received some attention, although opinions would be divided over the appropriateness of talking about guidelines and 'doctrines' here, as if the job of the theory was to advise people what to do. This approach has perhaps gone furthest in Bible translation, where there is a long tradition of guidelines and principles expressly designed to help future Bible translators. This seems to be the approach that you would like to see more of. Many scholars would prefer to think in terms of hypotheses or generalizations or probabilistic laws, based on observation.

EW

Most translators, on the other hand, would be happy to have some concrete advice and guidelines, even doctrines, as long as they are practical and realistic. It is regrettable that 'prescription' has been out of fashion in linguistics for the past few decades – the same decades that have seen the emergence of the would-be professional translator. Surely no profession can be based solely on observation and imitation of what other professionals do, plus a few probabilistic laws? Imagine a doctor or nurse newly arrived in a remote African country, faced by a malaria epidemic. What would they do? Just ask around and copy the others? Would they be expected to rediscover the aetiology of malaria, study the life cycle of the mosquito, and find a cure, without any guidance from their own theoretical training or from the research scientists and epidemiologists back home? These are all rhetorical questions, of course.

How can we translators lay claim to professional status, and assert ourselves as professionals rather than charlatans, if our research scientists fight shy of real-world problems and the advice that would help us to solve them? There seem to be no clear guidelines on how to select people for translator training, how to assess a translation, how to specify the purpose of a translation, how to measure and thus ensure reader satisfaction.

Translation theorists haven't even coined a comprehensible language in which we can talk about translation (surely the first step in moving up from faith-healer status?). Admittedly we do at least have two words, **translation** and **interpreting** to refer to the separate activities of translating the written word and interpreting the spoken word. But that's about as far as it goes. 'Translation' is a blanket term, used to refer to a huge range of activities and products. At the bottom end of the range, we find the tourist in a Greek supermarket, wondering whether that packet of white powder is sugar, salt, detergent or rat poison. When someone tells them which it is, that's a translation. And a very useful one too. Who wants to put rat poison in their coffee? At the top end of the range, we have Ted Hughes' translation of Aeschylus' *Oresteia*. There are many different products between the two extremes of 'Is-it-rat-poison?-translation' and 'Ted-Hughes-translation', and people often argue about them, because they expected one sort but were given the other. It has just happened again, here at the wordface. I spent part of this morning reading an exchange of e-mails with the Irish Association for Applied Linguistics about how to translate the European Year of Languages slogan *Languages open doors* into Irish. A literal translation would, it seems, be ugly and meaningless. Finally my colleague Donal Gordon came up with the wonderfully poetic translation *Teangacha – as ballaí fuinneoga* which means something like 'languages make walls into windows'. No sooner had I distributed the final list of translations than my Irish secretary Iseult popped her head round the door to say "Well, that's not a very good translation – *fuinneoga* means 'windows', not 'doors'..." Donal had provided a 'Ted-Hughes' translation; Iseult was looking for 'Is-it-rat-poison?'.

Couldn't translation theorists help us by defining some terms, so we can differentiate?

AC

You have a point, yes. In my view, one of the best contributions translation scholars can make to the work of professional translators is to study and then demonstrate the links between different translation decisions or strategies and the effects that such decisions or strategies seem to have on clients and readers and cultures, both in the past and in the present, under given conditions. Such corroborated correlations between cause and effect should be part of a professional's awareness: if I do this (e.g. if I correct this error in the source text), it is likely that, under these particular conditions / with this text-type etc., the effect will be such and such.

In the past, such correlations were simply assumed to justify prescriptive statements such as 'do this, don't do that'; it was believed that if such pre-scriptions were followed, good effects would ensue; if they were not followed, bad effects would ensue. In this way, translation norms arose, to be passed on as rules of thumb from teacher to apprentice, and from one translator to an-other. Such norms were usually assumed to be universal truths, but they were unfortunately often contradictory. Always translate as closely as you can to the original; always avoid translating too closely, word for word. Translate verse as verse; translate verse as prose. Your primary loyalty is to the original author; your primary loyalty is to your reader.

From the contemporary, empirical point of view, the problem with such prescriptive statements was that they were rarely explicitly tested. They often seemed to be no more than the projections of a particular scholar's beliefs, or a particular translator's opinions, generalized from a particular kind of trans-lation. If we can formulate such prescriptions as explicit hypotheses and then test them properly, we may get closer to being useful in the way you envis-age... We might even be able to find new hypotheses of cause and effect that had not been thought of before.

It is surely naive to expect that there should be somewhere, in some theo-rist's head, some kind of blanket advice that has universal applicability and just needs to be inscribed on a suitable stone tablet for instant use.

EW

It would certainly be naive to expect to find a single solution 'in some theo-rist's head'. For a start, there is often no single solution, but there might be a range of standard solutions. Secondly, I don't expect to find it in one person's head. In my view, 'theory' should not be just some individual's brain-child: it should arise from observing practice, analyzing practice, and drawing a few general conclusions to provide guidance. These conclusions should naturally be tested in practice. Leading to better guidance: better prescription based on better description.

Current medical practice for the treatment of malaria was not the brain-child of a single theorist; it resulted from years of observation and analysis, the identification of different types of malaria and corresponding treatments, practical clinical trails, constantly improved and adapted to circumstances (Hippocrates' advice to 'retire to the hills' not being practicable in all cases)... I'm sure all doctors and nurses know the standard ways of treating malaria, or could find out pretty fast – just as all lawyers know how to draw up different kinds of contract, and all architects know about different sorts of buildings. That's why we generally respect and depend on doctors, nurses, lawyers and architects. All I want is to put translators up there with respected professionals.

AC

Agreed. The big problem, I think, is that people have different opinions about what kind of a discipline translation theory actually is. Does it belong to the humanities? If so, we are presumably looking for greater understanding of what translations essentially are, the role translators play and have played in society and in intercultural relations, how some translated texts have enriched whole cultures, and how translators have sometimes been exploited for political and ideological ends, etc.

Or is it a more like a natural science? If so, we are looking for explanations of various kinds, just as we might seek explanations of any other natural phenomena. Why do translators tend to write more explicitly than their source-text authors? Why do translations often seem instantly recognizable as translations – how do they differ from parallel texts (non-translated texts of the same type)? Why do certain kinds of translations show more evidence of interference than other kinds? On what criteria do translators make their decisions? Even: why do clients often give translation jobs to non-native speakers of the target language? We might also be interested in studying the effects that translations have on their readers, and on the target cultures more generally. How do readers actually react to translations? How do they judge the acceptability of a translation? How can we measure translation effects? What do we discover if we compare client reactions with reader reactions?

Or is translation theory rather an applied science, with a research programme that starts with the need to solve particular problems or improve existing solutions? Professional translators seem to expect that this is what the theory should be doing. Well, general linguistic theory has helped to produce computer aids to translation – text-processing programs, spellcheckers, automatic dictionaries and thesauruses, termbases, translation management and workbench systems, computerized collections of parallel texts and previously translated texts, and then of course there is machine translation itself.

Apart from these concrete tools, what translation theory can also do is offer a set of conceptual tools. These can be thought of as aids for mental problem-solving, or for the development of the translator's self-image, or even for the enhancement of job satisfaction. At least, I hereby make this claim! When we get to the end of this book, you can decide whether the claim is justified or not...

EW

The conceptual tools sound interesting. Can they be used for problem-solving in the act of translation – to provide a toolkit of theoretical concepts that translators should bring to their job? For example, to solve the problem of dull, unreadable translation of the type shown below? This is a trap that many translators fall into with routine texts which they think 'don't matter'. Yet I would argue that everything matters, and there is no excuse for translating in this mechanistic way.

This example is a sentence from a European Commission recommendation on action to help 'SMEs' (small and medium-sized enterprises). This is a routine document addressed to politicians and bureaucrats, but even they deserve translations that are more readable than Translation A:

French original text:
Le rapport biannuel sur la coordination des activités en faveur des PME et de l'artisanat rendra compte des progrès accomplis notamment grâce à l'établissement et à la comparaison de données sur le taux de participation des PME aux programmes communautaires tant en nombre de projets qu'en volume budgétaire et à l'introduction, le cas échéant, de mesures spécifiques susceptibles d'augmenter la participation des PME.

Translation A:
The twice-yearly report on the coordination of activities to assist SMEs and the craft sector will detail the progress achieved, particularly through compiling and comparing data on the participation rate of SMEs in Community programmes – in terms both of the number of projects and the budgetary volume involved – and through the introduction, where appropriate, of special measures to increase the participation of SMEs.

A more readable translation would be something like this:

Translation B:
Our success or failure will be measured by the twice-yearly report on action to help small businesses. This will show exactly how many of them are involved in Community programmes – both the number of projects, and the financial volume they represent. The report will also chart the impact of any special measures that might boost applications from small businesses.

Which theoretical tools do you think Translator B used (consciously or otherwise) to arrive at Translation B instead of Translation A?

AC

Experienced professional translators use all kinds of conceptual tools in a routine way, without actually thinking of them, although they may have learned to use them consciously during their training. Here are some of the most common ones.

Transposition
This means changing the word class. 'Transposition' is one term used for this

idea (since Vinay and Darbelnet 1958), but different theorists use different names (sorry!). This seems to be an unknown idea to Translator A. True, that translator does try to get rid of a couple of nouns (... *the progress achieved, particularly through compiling and comparing data...*), but this only leads to a misinterpretation: it sounds as if the progress will be achieved by compiling data. Most of the French nouns come out faithfully as English nouns, and so on. But there is nothing sacred about word classes in texts like this. In English, verbal forms are generally preferable to the heavy abstract nouns so common in French, and introducing more verbs (as Translator B has done) makes it much easier to produce an acceptable version, less cluttered with nouns and prepositions. Translation A, on the other hand, is rather like what a good machine translation program could produce... What would your Systran program produce, I wonder?

EW

OK, here it is:

> **Raw Machine Translation:**
> The biannual report on the coordination of the activities for the SMEs and for the craft industry will give an account of the progress achieved in particular thanks to the establishment and thanks to the comparison of data on the rate of participation of the SMEs in the Community programmes both in number of projects and in budgetary volume and in the introduction, if necessary, of specific measures likely to increase the participation of the SMEs.

AC

Yes, no evidence of transposition here. Conceptual tools are, after all, only accessible to human brains – by definition! Strange, though, how some (less professional) translators seem to translate like machines. Here are some more useful concepts for human translators.

Deverbalization
This is a key term in the training used at the ESIT institute of interpretation and translation in Paris. It means simply that a translator or interpreter has to get away from the surface structure of the source text, to arrive at the intended meaning, and then express this intended meaning in the target language. (I will bypass here the deconstructionist arguments that there is no objective

meaning there in the first place. Translators have to believe that there is something there, after all...) In other words, deverbalization is a technique used to
avoid unwanted formal interference: professional translators need to process
the intended meaning in their own words, rather than try to mechanically
manipulate source-text structures. What has Translator A done? In most cases,
he or she seems to have processed the source structure bit by bit, twisting it
into some form of grammatical English, without stopping to ask what the hell
this is actually supposed to mean. I'd love to ask them: if you had this idea to
express in English, but no French source text to distract you, would you really express it like this? Are these words in the translation 'your own words'?
Would you really choose to have such a long subject? Would you yourself
use an expression like *the introduction, where appropriate*? Do you actually
like using such complicated noun phrases? More importantly: do you think
your readers find such a style pleasant to read, easy to understand?

Iconicity

Roughly speaking, iconicity is the matching of form and meaning, so that the
form reflects the meaning or the experience that is being described. It is a
well-known pragmatic maxim of clarity that iconic expressions are easier to
process than non-iconic ones. For instance, *Switch on after plugging in* is not
iconic. *Plug in before switching on* is iconic, because the order of information expressed matches the order of the events described.

Another aspect of iconicity is illustrated by your example: chunking, i.e.
the way the information / meaning / message is broken up into digestible
pieces. Translator B has chosen to split the French sentence into three chunks,
each encoding a distinct idea, so that the form (three sentences) reflects the
semantic structure: (1) there will be this report; (2) it will do this; and (3) it
will do that. Nice and clear.

Sometimes it can be difficult to find an iconic solution that can be combined with the need to deverbalize. So let's appeal to the concept of relevance.

Relevance

Readers of the translation will usually be different from the readers of the
original, and will have different cognitive backgrounds etc., they will have
different ideas about what is relevant to them. The translator's job is to translate what is relevant: this may mean explaining or adding or omitting things
occasionally. One scholar, Ernst-August Gutt (2000), puts the point in a way
that links it nicely with the deverbalization concept: what the translator has to
do in order to communicate successfully is to arrive at the intended interpretation of the original, and then determine in what respects the translation
should "interpretively resemble" the original in order to be consistent with
the principle of relevance for the target audience with its particular cognitive
environment. Other scholars have proposed a related concept: the maxim of

"sufficient degree of precision" (see Hönig and Kussmaul 1982; Schäffner 1998). Good professional translators go to the level of precision needed, not beyond it.

Another way of making this same point is to use the idea of **implicitation**. This conceptual tool is the technique of making information implicit: not everything needs to be explicit, not even everything that was explicit in the original. The opposite procedure is of course **explicitation**. There are examples of both in your French text:

Implicitation: *notamment grâce à l'établissement et à la comparaison de données sur* → (the report) will show (reports always do compile and compare data, so there is no need to say it)

Implicitation: *des PME et de l'artisanat* → small businesses (*artisanat* 'craft trades' can be omitted; show me a craftsman who's in BIG business)

Explicitation: *des progrès accomplis* → success or failure

Explicitation: PME → small businesses

But doesn't all this mean that the translation changes the style of the original? Well, in what respects should the style remain the same, do you think? If a translation (of a non-literary text) ends up being clearer than the original, so what? **Improving the original** is another useful concept.

EW

Yes – though not many translators have the confidence to suggest improving the original.

These 'conceptual tools' are excellent, and very interesting. So obviously translation theorists *can* help us, once they overcome their fear of being prescriptive. Why are these concepts useful? Because they provide labels for things that good translators do instinctively (at the same time 'coining a common language in which we can talk about translation', as I put it earlier). The guidelines embodied in transposition, deverbalization, iconicity and relevance are very sound.

I can't resist the urge to point out that a descriptive approach would not do anything to correct dull unreadable stuff like Translation A, which is typical of much of the output of bored professional translators with no self-esteem and a sneaking suspicion that no one will read their translation anyway. Translation B (produced by me) represents what I would have prescriptively instructed Translator A to produce if I'd had an opportunity to revise their translation. Did I use the tools of transposition, deverbalization, iconicity, relevance, explicitation and implicitation? Deverbalization, certainly (how can one translate without it?). Explicitation and implicitation are a conscious part of translation too. The others I obviously used subconsciously. Plus another tool (perhaps this comes under 'iconicity' or 'relevance') which was a desire to make the translation readable, by using more interesting words (*success, failure, impact, boost*) and shorter sentences (average sentence length: 20 words – another useful prescriptive guideline). Otherwise known as trying to keep the reader awake: 'desoporification'?

So what about the other problems plaguing translators – lack of confidence (arising from a poor self-image and uncertain professional status) and demotivation (caused by their invisibility and isolation, and the absence of feedback). Can you offer some solutions to those?

AC

Let's see...

2. Who am I? What am I doing?

EW

No translator would admit to suffering from an identity crisis. But that doesn't mean we don't have one. Hardly surprising, when the definition of 'translator' is so vague and the implications of 'translation' vary so widely. At one end of the scale there is the translator-slave, still alive and well and receiving instructions to 'just type this out in English'. At the other we find the martyr William Tyndale, burned at the stake in 1536 for translating the Bible into English, and his modern counterparts, the Italian, Japanese and Norwegian translators killed or injured for translating Salman Rushdie's *Satanic Verses*.[1]

Can translation theory help us here? Are there any useful generalizations that would provide us with viable role models somewhere between these two extremes?

AC

Translators' role models have indeed changed and varied enormously throughout history. Scholars have been interested in this, both in translators' self-concepts and in their public image in the eyes of others. One line of investigation has been to explore the all-too-revealing metaphors that have been used for this (a list of metaphors can be found in Koller 1972: 40f; others are discussed in my book, Chesterman 1997: Ch. 2).

In antiquity, for instance, one of the dominant images of the translator was that of a *builder*: his (usually it was his, not her) task was to carefully demolish a building, a structure (the source text), carry the bricks somewhere else (into the target culture), and construct a new building – with the same bricks. The bricks thus represented some kind of minimum chunks of meaning, and the assumption was that these remained constant. Language was thought to be a mirror of reality, so there was a one-to-one correspondence between bits of the world and bits of language, which meant that the rebuilding project could go ahead without being impeded by philosophical doubts. A modern version of the same metaphor is the image of someone going through customs: they are asked to unpack all their clothes and transfer them to another suitcase. Same clothes, different packaging. Both versions thus hang on to

---

[1] Hitoshi Igarashi, a Japanese scholar who translated Salman Rushdie's *Satanic Verses*, was stabbed to death in July 1991. Italian translator Ettore Caprioli was wounded in a knife attack the same month. In October 1993, Norwegian translator William Nygaard was shot three times and seriously wounded. Source: <http://www.messiah.org/p13404.htm> (Quotation from *Chicago Tribune,* Section 1, Friday, September 25, 1998, p. 20.)

the notion of keeping something the same, unchanged, constant, through a process of change. This certainly captures one aspect of translation – but there have of course been arguments about what 'same' means here, whether this 'sameness' can actually exist, and whether it is reasonable to detach meaning from language in this way. We will come back to these arguments later.

By the way, I find your own metaphor of the wordface / coalface fascinating, but depressing. It seems to carry some provocative connotations: hard manual work, underground in a dark place, perhaps in a cramped space, surrounded by noise, where people get covered with dust; they dig away at the linguistic ground-rock in search of a valuable mineral (meaning?) which lies hidden there, a mineral that has been deposited over a long period and has become fossilized; teamwork, poorly paid. You certainly do not seem to be worried about preserving sameness – in fact at the wordface you are chipping holes in what would have otherwise remained unchanged – 'the same' – if you had not interfered!

Are these the associations you want me to have?

EW

Preserving sameness is a fundamental part of our job, of course... that goes without saying. And the way we do it is quite straightforward. When I am translating, I just think: 'If President Prodi had given this speech in English, what would he have said?' 'If this German article on embryology had been written in English, what would it have said?' Our job is to find the right words to convey information and express ideas that are not our own.

I suppose we talk about 'working at the wordface' because for us, translation is production-line writing under constraints: constraints of deadline, form and language. We're not 'chipping holes in something' – and nor is the miner. He is getting valuable coal out of a difficult and inaccessible place and loading it (day in, day out) onto a conveyor belt that takes it up to the surface, where the people who need it can make use of it. We wordface workers sit in front of our PC screens and laboriously prise the right words out of our subconscious or our memory banks or wherever. Then we send them off for someone else to use somewhere. The parallel with mining can't be taken too far: miners work under much more difficult, noisy and dangerous conditions than we do. But metaphors shouldn't be taken too literally, should they?

Same problem with the 'translator as builder': it's a good image, but surely (if I may be nit-picking) builders use new materials, not something recovered from a demolition site? If they did, they would destroy the original in the process. That wouldn't go down too well with President Prodi. Perhaps I've missed the point. Any more good metaphors?

AC

Another dominant metaphor in early thinking on translation a dominant metaphor was *copying*. The foremost translators and theorists of this stage (in the

West) were involved in the translation of religious texts, primarily of the Bible into Latin. In holy texts, it was felt, even the form was holy. To meddle with the original form of the scriptures was to risk blasphemy. One solution was to supply a (maximally) literal translation, 'word-for-word' but preserving target-language grammaticality. It was accepted that the translators would have to make some formal or structural changes during the process of translation, but these were to be kept to a minimum.

Translators themselves had no authority; they were totally subservient to the source text. They were humble copiers: deviation from the original was a sin. This approach was motivated in the first place by fear, the fear of heresy and its consequences. It was also motivated by a respect for the authority of the source text that originated in its worship. In the Renaissance, Erasmus wrote that he preferred "to sin through excessive scrupulousness rather than through excessive license" (in Lefevere (trans.) 1992b: 60), i.e. to translate too literally rather than too freely.

Although this approach seems to have started life in the context of biblical translation, it spread to other contexts in which the form of the original text was somehow felt to be particularly significant: philosophy, scientific and technical texts. Reverence for the source text, and the consequent insistence on literal translation, is also evident in the ideas of some modern literary translators. Nabokov is a good example.

EW

With all due respect to Nabokov, this reminds me of the 'reverence' (or lack of confidence) we see in newly recruited translators who are overawed by the subject matter. Too scared to admit that they don't really understand a text, they translate it literally in the hope that the Real Experts will be able to make something out of it.

Even experienced translators will sometimes resort to literal or word-for-word translation to elucidate certain phrases or passages. And there are some cases where it is preferable to 'sin through excessive scrupulousness', for example when translating legislation. In some EEC Regulations on fishing quotas, the French expression *poissons sortis de la mer* was translated into English as *fish caught*; but many legal wrangles could have been avoided if it had been translated literally as *fish taken out of the sea*. It has become clear that fishermen are quite capable of catching fish in one place and taking them out of the sea in a different one (having towed the catch into different territorial waters if that is to their advantage). But of course literal translation or 'copying' is quite unsuitable for most text types.

AC

Yes, one of the first scholars to make the link between translation method and text type was Jerome, who himself translated both religious texts and literary classics. He argued that non-sacred texts should be translated more freely. So from copying, we shift to *imitating*. Imitating requires its own creative force, even a virtuoso sense of 'I can do that better than you can'. Translators begin to assume more authority, more responsibility for the authorship of their translation.

Jerome, the patron saint of translators, lived c.342-420. He was a brilliant scholar and a prolific translator of Christian texts, most famously the Vulgate, the Latin translation of the Bible that remained the definitive version until the Reformation. When criticized for his translations by St Augustine, because they changed traditional wordings in places, he is said to have replied that "God is on the side of the scholar".

During the Middle Ages, vernacular translations of poetry and prose were often very free indeed, and raised the perennial question of how free a translation can get before it becomes something other than a translation, such as an adaptation. Even biblical translation came under the influence of this new approach: Luther took great care to make his German translation fit naturally into the vernacular, so that its function should be more effectively served. Clarity, intelligibility, readability, fluency – these were the things that mattered.

This tradition reached its height during the neo-classical period, when very free translations of literary works were fashionable in some countries. In France, these were famously known as *belles infidèles*. (Sorry to be sexist... It is interesting, though, that translations have often been thought of as 'female', in contrast to 'male' originals; female, and therefore secondary, of lesser value, subservient, shining only with a reflected light, etc.This is one aspect that modern feminist translators and theorists have been highlighting, and resisting.)

The priority in this 'imitation' idea was to please the reader, and closeness to the source text was played down (we are talking about literary translation, here); this was sometimes taken to astonishing extremes, with translators bowdlerizing source texts quite freely in the interests of producing a target text that would be thought suitably uplifting..., or which would sell well.

Belles infidèles

This term was first applied to the translations of Nicolas Perrot d'Ablancourt, in 17th-century France. His translations of classical Latin and Greek authors were intended to please the French public, to conform to the fashionable French ideals of elegance and good taste. This approach to translation became something of a norm in France for a long period: the

---

foreign, the Other, was made French, domesticated, adapted and even improved when necessary. In the preface to his translation of Lucian, d'Ablancourt writes that "there are also passages in which I have considered what ought to be said, or what I could say, rather than what he actually said" (as translated by André Lefevere 1992b: 37). In justifying his way of translating, he says: "what I have produced is certainly not a translation, properly speaking. It is better than a translation [...]".

EW

Of course reader-friendliness is still an important consideration, fighting the fog of obfuscation etc.; but nowadays we don't expect translators to act as censors as well, picking and choosing the content that will not insult the feelings of their readers.

AC

Or do we? One recent metaphor that appeals to some postmodernist scholars is that of the translator as a *cannibal*, consuming the flesh of (presumably dead) writers in order to benefit from their strength. As cannibals, translators take and eat what they please, and do with their source text what they please, with the sole purpose of benefiting the target culture. Source texts are mere food, to be digested and exploited at will. So, for instance, you might translate the New Testament in such a way that it appears as a pamphlet in defence of the Black Liberation movement, with Christ speaking like a radical activist (see Chapter 6, below). Personally, I think this is valid translation, so long as the translator states explicitly to the readers, e.g. in a preface, what the overall translation strategy is, so that they know what to expect. Such an explicit statement also makes the translator visible.

EW

But perhaps too visible? This metaphor – call it 'imitation' if you like, but 'cannibalism' sounds closer – all seems very far from the wordface to me. Translators who exhibit any tendency to distort a source text for their own religious or political ends will not get far. Another point is this: we are not usually dealing with dead authors who can be plagiarized or bowdlerized at will. Our authors are very much alive, and many have opinions (often misinformed, it's true) about how our translations should read. In day-to-day practice, for example in international organizations producing political documents, even our texts are not dead. They are evolving from first draft via many rewrites to the final version, and translation plays a part in that process. The 'authors' (usually committees) need translation to help them perfect the document, but the political aspects are far more important to them, and they don't want us to get in the way or delay the process. Translators have to play their part in this process by rendering the political nuances of the original text as faithfully as possible.

AC

Obviously both over-literalism and excesses of free imitation had their dangers, and a new approach was needed. This new attitude emerged particularly in literary translation during the German Romantic period. An early expression comes in Schleiermacher's argument against imitation in his essay *Über die verschiedenen Methoden des Übersetzens* in 1813 (in Robinson 1997a). Imitation, like copying, is ultimately impossible, he argues, and mere paraphrase destroys the spirit of the original. In place of these, instead of carrying the translation to the reader, the translation of literature should aim at a style that is deliberately marked, strange, foreign, so that the reader feels the translation to be unfamiliar and is thus moved back towards the original; the experience should be as if a foreign spirit were blown towards the reader. The translator thus had an important role in enriching readers by exposing them to foreign influences that were outside their normal reading experience.

So during the Romantic period, translators were very visible indeed. We find images that highlight more of the translator's *creative* role, like that of a performing artist or musician, giving a performance (a rendering) of the original score. As creative writers, translators were given a major role to play in developing young cultures, strengthening feelings of national identity, encouraging the extension of literary genres and extending the target language. They did this partly by translating in such a way that the translations were overtly translations, rather than 100% natural target language. Instead, the idea was to allow the source text somehow to shine through, so that both source and target languages were visible at the same time, producing a kind of hybrid style. In other words, they deliberately exploited interference from the source text, and deliberately used an unusual style, unusual structures and vocabulary, in the target language itself. Here again, of course, we are talking about literary translation only. It is actually rather striking that a great deal of what has passed as traditional translation theory has in fact been restricted to literary translation.

EW

Yes, that may be why most translators reject traditional translation theory as irrelevant. Unfortunately – and I hope you can prove that translation theory (traditional or otherwise) is relevant... For how can we practising translators expect to be taken seriously, as fully-fledged professionals, or even reach a consensus among ourselves, if we can't provide any sort of systematic theoretical basis for our choices and demands?

As for the metaphor of translation as 'creating': I'm sure that many of my colleagues do see themselves as creative artists, and would recognize themselves in the image you've just given: 'a performing artist or musician, giving a performance (a rendering) of the original score'.

However, the idea of a hybrid style allowing the foreign text to shine though the translation sounds a bit dodgy. Strictly for literary translation, after all... not something we would deliberately aim for in the non-fiction department (although unfortunately it can happen by mistake, when working under pressure to meet a deadline). The reproach we fear most is this: 'It reads like a translation'.

AC

With the advent of modern information theory and the computer age we then find images of *decoding and recoding*, and the picture of the creative human translator seems to dwindle, to be replaced by that of the robotic brain, processing bits of information. There is a famous quote by Weaver (1955:18), one of the founders of cybernetics, to this effect: "One naturally wonders if the problem of translation could conceivably be treated as a problem in cryptography. When I look at an article in Russian, I say: This is really written in English, but it has been coded in some strange symbols. I will now proceed to decode".

This metaphor certainly does not highlight the translator's visibility. Rather, it dehumanizes the translator into something mechanical. Is this what you feel like, down there at the wordface?

EW

Not really, no. Quite frankly, some of us like being in the backroom. Not everyone strives for stardom. But your metaphor of 'translation as transcoding' is certainly something we recognize: the common misconception (aided and abetted by the advent of machine translation) that translation is just a matter of pressing a button and out will come the right words in another language. Yet it is perfectly clear, especially to those of us who work with machine translation, that real translation is a different matter. Machines can certainly help, and they have transformed the way we work; and our contact with machine translation has forced us to think harder and more systematically about what 'real translation' is, and why it is different from anything a machine can do without human assistance. We'll come back to this in Chapter 7.

AC

Perhaps as a reaction against this mechanical picture, the following major stage stressed the human aspects of *communication*, with the translator acting as a mediator, sending on a message, responsive to the needs of the sender, the original writer, and the potential readers (see, for example, Nord 1997). Translating is designing a text, for a particular purpose; the source text is one input for this design, but only one: other considerations also affect the final translation. Scholars working with this approach tend to stress the role of the translator as an expert, a communication expert. This expertise includes not only translating itself, in the strict sense, but all the other aspects of multilingual documentation and resource management as well. So the translator's status seems to grow again.

Eugene Nida, for instance (a highly influential Bible translator and linguist), talks about the need to consider the reader's reactions, and to focus on getting the same effect as the original, rather than the same form (see Nida 1964; Nida and Taber 1969). In an application of information theory, he discusses how, in translation, redundancy may have to be added in order to guarantee that the message gets through in spite of noise in the channel. Another aspect he analyzes is the way looser structures (e.g. with more finite verbs) are easier to understand than very dense ones (with more nouns and a thick cluster of modification before the main noun) that burden the short-term memory too much. Looser structures flow through the communication channel more easily. Compare:

(a) *multipartner and multinational shared-cost research and technological development projects*
vs.
(b) *multipartner and multilateral projects that share the costs of research and technological development.*

Which do you find easier to read?

EW

OK, no contest. Here at last is an image that most of us industrial-scale practitioners would accept. Translation is all about communication – we are mediators, and regardless of our own feelings or boredom threshold, we try to convey the message of the source text to the potential readers of that sort of text. In the process we take account of the context of the original and the purpose for which it was written, and we try to render it as effectively as possible in the way that a similar text would have been written in the target language. There are many ways in which theorists could help us here: firstly by producing a usable text typology, and then a hierarchy of translation functions and loyalties. It is not always possible to be loyal to both the original writer *and* the readers. Sometimes it has to be one or the other.

For example, imagine you are asked to translate a letter from a job applicant, and it contains some misprints or inconsistencies. If your loyalty is to the company that may be recruiting the applicant, you will translate in a way that shows up the mistakes. But if you were translating the same letter for friend who's trying to get a job, you would translate it differently.

AC

Yes, the purpose of the translation is a crucial factor. One modern theory of translation makes this idea its cornerstone: this is the **skopos** theory.

> *Skopos* is the Greek for aim or purpose. The skopos theory of translation is associated primarily with German scholars following Hans J. Vermeer. This theory sees translation primarily as action: human agents act in a rational way, and their actions are governed by their intentions. Every act, including acts of translation, has a skopos. It is the skopos that determines what kind of relationship there should be between source and target text. The same source text, translated with two different *skopoi*, will give rise to different kinds of translation. The theoretical problem then is to plot the correspondences between the skopos and the translator's textual decisions in practice (see Nord 1997).

A focus on the skopos and on the intended effect of the translation, means that correspondingly less priority will be given to the original source text. Ideas of *equivalence* as a desirable goal give way to those of *functional adequacy*.

EW

This preoccupation with the target text is reflected in one aspect of professional practice that is almost universal today: translators normally translate into their mother tongue. So even if the translation is inaccurate, it will at least be well-written.

AC

Another approach focussing on the target culture rather than the source text emerged from comparative literary studies in the 1970s and 1980s. This work started from the premise that translations are facts within the target culture, so *that* is where translation scholarship should start too, not with the translator looking at a source text and wondering what to do. This target-oriented approach has its roots in the work of the Israeli scholars Itamar Even-Zohar and Gideon Toury, but their ideas were quickly taken up by scholars in the Netherlands, Belgium and the UK.

These scholars look at the ways in which (usually literary) translations have been received in the target culture, what effects these translations have had, and why they have been received in this way. A central concept is that of the **norm**, defined as a social notion of correctness. The job of the translation scholar is to discover the norms in the target culture that affect the reception of the translation, and also the norms in the source culture that maybe also affected the way the text was translated. Insofar as translators have knowledge of these norms, and themselves accept them, norms thus offer ways of explaining why translations (of a given type, into a given culture at a given time) look the way they do. Norms have a prescriptive force that regulates the translator's decisions.

Norms are not permanent laws, however; they can be broken, perhaps to be replaced by better norms. How, why and when norms change is an interesting question. Under what circumstances do translators feel that they can begin to break norms? Norm-breaking may lead to criticism, but it may also lead to better norms.

The target-oriented approach has also highlighted issues of translator power: translators are seen as manipulators, gate-keepers between cultures (see Hermans 1985). Their actions affect not only target-culture readers but the target culture in general, and also intercultural relations in general.

Translators have acted as censors, they have twisted texts in accordance with the wishes of their client, or indeed their own wishes (recall the cannibal image we mentioned earlier).

EW

The idea of translators as gate-keepers between cultures seems rather quaint to me, and again applicable only to literary translation. No one denies that literary translators do enrich different cultures by 'unlocking' inaccessible works. And I can see how their activity could be seen as manipulation, because they influence our perception of the other culture... But when we leave the realm of literature, and enter the non-fiction zone, I think translators have a different role. The international organizations that employ many of us non-fiction translators occupy a supranational space in which language matters very little as long it doesn't inhibit communication. That is: as long as translations are provided rapidly enough for the organization to be able to function in the same way as it would if it were monolingual; and as long as we tolerate some non-standard use of the *lingua franca*. Eventually this tolerance – or laxity – can in fact inhibit communication. Take Eurospeak, for example: a language widely spoken and written within the EU institutions but incomprehensible to most of the general public. Here translators are not cultural gate-keepers but cultural referees, reminding players of the rules, and showing the red card to offenders whose bad habits threaten to cause a breakdown in communication.

AC

From your point of view, as a translator in the EU institutions, I can see that the idea of moving texts from one culture to another seems a bit odd: for you, concepts of source and target cultures are blurred by the fact that much of your translation work is intracultural, within a multicultural or multilingual whole, as it were.

Another special feature of EU translation is the strange myth you have to accept, that officially there is no source text and no target text because, whatever actually happens chronologically, all the language versions are of equal legal status. (A bit like Orwell's point that all animals are equal, but some are more equal than others?) I can see why this is a necessary belief – just as I can see why you therefore need to believe in the illusion of 'perfect equivalence' – i.e. 'identity' – between the different versions. But if you look at translation activities as a whole, through history, I think you will find that this kind of situation is exceptional. (It may of course become less exceptional as time goes on.)

Some of your translations are nevertheless meant for the external reader, the general public, not some EU-internal receiver. In this case, the cultural shift is from the EU culture to, say, the Spanish or Finnish culture: your target readers are then addressed as members of these cultures rather than as members of the multilingual EU culture.

Does this get forgotten sometimes, or do your translators automatically assume they are addressing EU insiders?

EW

No, but sometimes our subject matter is such that it only makes sense to people who understand the internal workings of the European Union's institutions. Not everyone does, or wants to do so. In my opinion there is nothing intrinsically different about translating for the EU institutions. There are many other international organizations where translation is done in similar circumstances and for similar reasons (such as the United Nations and its agencies, the World Bank, the OECD, Nordic Council, NATO, Council of Europe... I could go on). Then there are the multinational companies, banks, law firms, hardware and software producers, big pharmaceutical and chemical companies – all of these employ professional translators, either as staff translators in-house or on a freelance basis.

It would make for greater professional solidarity if we, as translators, could stop dividing our profession up into sectors and factions: in-house versus freelance, public-sector versus private-sector, and so on. Yes, there are differences: but some are imagined ones, based on mutual resentment and non-existent perks. Freelances envy us in-house translators because we don't have to worry where the next job, or the next pay packet, will be coming from. We wage slaves envy freelance translators because they are free: free to say 'no' to boring jobs, unreasonable deadlines, and offensive customers, whereas we have no choice. But let's not dwell on these differences. In any case, the distinction between the public and private sector is blurred by the fact that so many translators work in both, at different stages of their careers. The public sector is not a different planet: much public-sector translation (including EU translation) is done by freelances and private-sector translation companies. For the purposes of this discussion, I'd prefer to concentrate on what we translators have in common, not on what separates us. Because if we don't hang together, we will hang separately.

One of the things professional translators have in common is this: when working on non-fiction texts, as opposed to literary ones, we occasionally have to translate badly written material. So even if the content or message is not very clearly or attractively expressed in the original text, it must nevertheless be correctly conveyed in another language. Sometimes in several other languages, in which case the translations must all say the same (obviously). And in organizations like the EU institutions, the translations continue to co-exist with each other and with the original, unlike literary translations. If our texts are 'moved' into a national culture and cease to look the same, or at least fairly similar, some countries will complain about unequal treatment. We do occasionally get suspicious readers asking why 'their' text is shorter than the French or German one – does this mean, they ask, that they are being short-changed? Has some imagined privilege been reserved for the other Member States?

AC

I agree that the metaphor of movement is not really appropriate: texts actually do not move from one place to another during translation, not at least in the sense that when they arrive at place B they are gone from place A. Rather, they duplicate, become replicated, spread, spawning copies (or, I would say, variants) of themselves in other languages. Sometimes these variants seem to be more like mutants, which is when things get really interesting.

Despite your suspicion of the weird ideas of theorists focussing on literary translation, you might in fact find that some of the postmodern ideas about translation fit the EU situation rather well. Some postmodern/ deconstructivist thinkers (like Derrida, for instance) stress that all texts are fundamentally intertextual, they are built up of words and expressions that have been used a million times before. This means that no one can really claim to be an 'original' writer, because all a writer does is cut-and-paste from the already-existing universe of texts. In fact, the whole idea of the author has been demoted by postmodernists: the author is not an authority, the author is dead, all we have is texts. Outside the texts – nothing. Further: meanings are not fixed but endlessly shifting and deferred, all is indeterminate, everyone interprets a text in their own way: this means that any notion of equivalence goes out of the window, since there is nothing 'objectively there' that can be equivalent to anything else. There is no 'centre'.

This view gives the translator enormous freedom, of course (recall the cannibal image again). If the author is dead, and the source text therefore is not a sacred authority, the translator is free to play... One recurrent postmodern metaphor is that of the carnival (see Oittinen 1993). In a carnival, existing values and statuses are turned upside down, the prevailing order is upset, authors are dead – so long live the translators!

As long as the translators are king and queen, they are guaranteed high visibility at least. Many contemporary writers on translation highlight this theme – that the translator should not hide beneath the text but be visible in it... (and outside it too).

EW

Somewhat unrealistic, sorry. It is not particularly helpful for theorists to tell us that translation is impossible or that perfect equivalence is unattainable. Let alone that words are meaningless and there is nothing objectively there.

I hope that when Madame Derrida sends her husband to the super-market with a shopping list marked with the words *filets de sole, beurre, farine* and he comes back with some paper clips and a packet of Gauloises, she hits him over the head with the frying pan.

There is always something objectively there, an intention underlying the expression... and translators have to decide what it is, dig it out and put it into a usable and approximately equivalent form.

AC

The whole idea of a single source-text author must sometimes seem tricky in your situation, doesn't it? And sometimes you have to translate texts for no real readers, just in order that the text can then be said to exist in another language? The EU bureaucracy as a whole sometimes appears (to us outsiders) to correspond surprisingly well to the postmodern picture of a world consisting entirely of texts, divorced from writers, readers, reality...

EW

In the EU institutions we often don't have a single source-text author, but a committee or a succession of committees. We never translate for 'no real readers' (we try to be optimistic); we don't translate just for insiders, but for the outside world too; and we don't translate everything into all official languages. We choose the languages of translation on the basis of the target readership. If a text is for national representatives or the European public (e.g. legislation and reports) then we translate into all 11 official languages. If it's for insiders, then we translate into English or French. If it's for one particular country or member of the public (e.g. a reply to an enquiry), then we translate into the one language required. I hope all this has restored your faith in the EU bureaucracy, at least as far as translation is concerned.

It seems clear that we, like thousands of fellow translators working for scores of similar organizations, do in fact have lots of roles to play – occasionally copying or imitating, creating if we're lucky, sometimes decoding and recoding, more often communicating, perhaps a spot of manipulating (but I hope never cannibalizing). I think we do almost all of these at different times, depending on the nature and purpose of the text we're translating. And it is useful to be made more conscious of the fact.

3. I translate therefore I am not

AC

> Book translators are campaigning for recognition, seeking to have their names on the covers of books rather than buried inside in the small print. The men and women who help to make some of the world's great literature accessible feel they have been overshadowed and undervalued for too long.

This is the beginning of a piece in *The Times* of December 2, 1998 entitled 'A talent lost in translation' by Dalya Alberge. The context was the 1998 Nobel Prize for Literature that was awarded to the Portuguese writer Jose Saramago, and the fact that few members of the press or the general public appeared to realize that his novels could only be read by most people, including the Nobel jury, because they had been translated. "You had to look pretty hard to find any mention of Giovanni Pontiero, the translator who enabled most of the world to read *The Year of the Death of Ricardo Reis*".

"Translators are perceived as an invisible agent", David Constantine pointed out in the same article. Another translator suggested that "there is a sort of conspiracy within the publishing world to pretend that the book hasn't been translated". Some publishers apparently fear that if a (literary) book is advertised as a translation, people will not buy it...

I wonder how widespread this feeling is among other kinds of translators – this feeling of invisibility, of not being seen or appreciated. I recall your wordface metaphor again: there you are, burrowing away underground, out of sight... Who even knows that you are there? How do you think non-literary translators feel about this issue? Do they too want to see their names mentioned on the texts they translate, do they feel that they are not recognized?

EW

Yes, we feel that we are not recognized; but no, we don't think that having our names on our translations would solve the problem. Really there are two problems: lack of appreciation (which is not the same thing as personal visibility), and lack of professional recognition.

Naturally we would agree that literary translators deserve to have their names on the cover with the author's – in smaller print, of course. The same rule should perhaps apply to any non-literary texts that have a named author (I noticed that the five intrepid German translators who translated the massive Starr Report on the Clinton/Lewinsky scandal were duly named in the German version that was published an astounding ten days after the original). But most non-literary texts are different. When did you last see a law or an instruction booklet or even a political speech published with the name of the real author on it? The authors are anonymous civil servants or technical writers or political advisers who are just as invisible as we are. Often, too, there is no single author or translator; these texts are a collective or corporate product, not a personal exercise in creativity.

In any case most translators are shy and retiring creatures. Our job is to be invisible and neutral, not to distort the original text by imposing our own personality on it. Don't you think it's our duty to stay out of sight?

AC

There is certainly a problem here. In translation studies there have been discussions (occasionally quite anguished ones) from various points of view. One recurring image of translation that we didn't mention earlier is that of a window, or a pane of glass. In order to see the original text properly, as it really is, the translation has to be transparent, so that the eye does not rest on the glass itself but looks through it, imagining that what it sees is really the original, with nothing intervening. The translation (and hence the translator who produced it) is therefore literally invisible. If, on the other hand, the translation is like a stained-glass window, the eye rests on the patterned surface and does not look through it.

If this is indeed the way you see yourself, and also the way others see you, then you certainly do risk turning into 'the invisible man'. (Remember the wonderful novel by Ralph Ellison (1952), about the way blacks feel when whites 'look through them' as if they were not there? No identity, no right to exist, mere nothing.)

This image has various consequences. At the purely linguistic level, it seems to follow that the ideal style for any translation is total native-speaker fluency. No specks of interference or clumsiness or ungrammaticality must be left on the glass, to impede the reader's eye.

You can see something of this assumption in the way research on translation errors has developed (see *TTR* 1989; House 1997; Reiss 2000). Originally, we looked at obvious **overt** errors, classified them, and tried to suggest causes and ways of avoiding them. Basic categories were:

* equivalence – 'not the same meaning';
* form – ungrammatical structure;
* style – not the same style as the original; 'clumsy, unnatural style'; even 'reads like a translation' – the ultimate criticism!;
* effect – does not have the same effect as the original did on the original readers.

More recently, however, the availability of big computer corpora has led to an interest in what have been called **covert** or **distribution** or **quantitative** errors (see Kenny 1999; Laviosa-Braithwaite 1998). These are things like using a given word or structure much more often, or less often, than it would be used by native speakers writing a text of a similar sort on the same kind of subject. Scholars compare translations with such **parallel texts** in order to discover what marks translations as translations, if anything. Are there too many adjectives? Is the average sentence length too long? What about the distribution of finite verbs?

This kind of research tells us something about universal features of translations, whatever the languages involved. It seems, for instance, that translators anywhere tend to use more standardized language than comparable target-language texts. Their texts have a narrower, more prototypical distribution of different linguistic features, and do not make so much use of less frequent forms. The style thus often turns out to be a bit 'flat'. (Of course, there are exceptions: these are general trends only.)

This kind of information can also be useful for translators who want to refine their use of the target language and make it more similar to non-translated texts of the same kind, who want to produce more 'natural' translations. If you know that translators tend to do X, but actually you would not like to do X, you can try to guard against it.

The implication seems to be that ideal translations – at least, of the kind studied in this research, such as those that you find in your daily newspaper – would be totally fluent, totally transparent, they would fit exactly into the relevant family of target-language texts and be unrecognizable as translations. Translations must not be seen to be different, in any way! But they are different of course, and that is why we find it interesting to study them.

For some kinds of texts, the following rule-of-thumb seems to hold: if readers suspect at any point that they are reading a translation, then there must be something wrong with it. Or: if computer analysis can discover any significant quantitative difference between a translation and a relevant set of parallel texts (original, not translated), then there must be something wrong with the translation.

Now, this ideal clearly does not hold for all kinds of translation. When you read a Russian novel in English, you know that it is not really an English novel, that it is a translation. So, probably, are the instructions for setting up your video recorder, and a hundred other translation types. So this 'linguistic invisibility' is not a universal ideal for all translation. One problem is that is it often mistakenly assumed to apply universally. Historically, the ideal has been associated e.g. with Renaissance ideas of translation as 'imitation', as we mentioned in the previous chapter.

EW

You've mentioned two situations that may make translators visible: when the translation is bad (errors, unnatural style, etc.), so the reader concludes that 'it must be a translation'; and when the original text (Russian novel, etc.) was obviously written in another language so, again, 'it must be a translation'.

There are other cases, too, where the translator may have to come out of hiding, for example by appending a translator's note to explain why a text has had to be adapted during translation in order to achieve the purpose of the original.

An obvious example of the visible translator is the translator-scholar dealing with texts that are culturally or historically remote, needing detailed commentaries, introductions and footnotes to get the message of the original across to the reader. These translators are often academic specialists in their own right, rather than 'mere' translators, and well able to articulate the problems of translation generally. It was in Robin Waterfield's preface to the Penguin edition of Plato's *Philebus* that I found this astute observation:

> The style of Plato's *Philebus* is occasionally turgid, the meaning often far from clear. Both sorts of obscurity are the province of the translator. My policy as regards the stylistic density has been to try and make the dialogue readable; but at some points I have found it impossible not to reproduce the somewhat stilted nature of the Greek, especially where this occurs in the first place for the sake of philosophical completeness. Obscurity of meaning, on the other hand, is usually impossible to remove by fair translation. Yet the translator has to understand the text in order to provide a meaningful translation. Consequently, as has often been remarked, any translation of a complex work is bound to reflect partisan views of certain passages: *traduttore traditore*. (Waterfield 1982:7)

AC

You quote the translator's urge to 'make the dialogue readable' – suggesting a kind of inner compulsion towards clarity, a resistance to obfuscation. This illustrates a specific hypothesis that has been much explored recently, the **explicitation hypothesis**.

The explicitation hypothesis claims that translators universally tend to make things explicit, more explicit than they were in the source text. You can see this in the way translators tend to dislike ambiguities and unclear structures, the way they use pronouns and connectors, the way they tend to add explanations to obscure or culture-bound terms, the way things that were implicit in the original often become more explicit in the translation, and so on.

I wonder what Waterfield means by 'fair translation', though? Don't you think that translators do indeed tend to reduce obscurity (not necessarily always, with all types of text, granted)? They have to understand the source text, as you say; and it is their own understanding that they then seek to pass on. Literally: they pass on what has become clear to them. The explicitation hypothesis seems intuitively very reasonable – even self-evident, when you come to think of it.

EW

Yes, our job is to communicate, to help the reader to understand; so we do often make the text more explicit. If the reader can't understand, we'll be blamed. Technical and bureaucratic writing is often turgid, and the image of the organization may suffer if we translators don't tidy it up a bit. The original may contain mistakes that we would try to correct in translation, rather than perpetuating them. (Of course there are some rare situations – translating exam answers and project proposals, for example – where producing a 'fair translation' means resisting the temptation to try and improve the original.)

It is an interesting problem: what to do when the original contains mistakes. I am not talking about ethics here, where the translator disagrees with the author's moral or political standpoint, but about mistakes on basic points of fact: incorrect dates, missing words, inaccurate quotations. This is surely another case where translators have to speak with their own voice, either to the author (asking to get the original corrected) or to the reader (with a translator's note or a 'sic')?

Dealing with errors in the original makes translators visible, challenges the author's authority, and can pose a problem of professional credibility. I'm thinking of typical errors of this kind:

> ... *Mrs Thatcher, the famous socialist leader...*
> ... *since the Second World War ended in 1939...*
> ... *the maximum permitted dose is 3 x 10 mg tablets or 300 mg per day*

Assuming the translator notices the error, he or she has five choices:

1. do nothing, just translate;
2. translate literally but put in a [sic];
3. correct covertly (translate correctly but don't draw attention to the error);
4. correct overtly (translate correctly and put in a translator's note drawing attention to the error in the original);
5. correct fully: translate it correctly and get the original corrected too.

There is, of course, no blanket solution. But there is surely a way of applying the solutions systematically, depending on the type of document and other factors. In a multilingual organization where a text is being translated into several languages at the same time, and all the translations will co-exist with the original, it is actually quite important to ensure that all the translators do the same thing. And that they don't *all* phone the author to ask what she or he really meant to say. (Let's assume, for the sake of simplicity, that for once there *is* a single author responsible.)

The errors I've mentioned may seem easy to correct, but you'd be surprised.

Example: ... *Mrs Thatcher, the famous socialist leader...*
Translator to author's secretary: Mr X has written that Mrs Thatcher is a socialist. Can I correct that to say 'Conservative'?
Author's secretary: Well he doesn't like being disturbed. Can't you just

translate it?

Translator: But Mrs Thatcher isn't a socialist. She's a Conservative.

Secretary: He's a world authority you know. Perhaps he was using socialist in a special sense...?

Translator: Can't I just have a word with him?

Author to translator (after explanation of problem): Whoops! Thanks for
pointing it out. That might have caused a diplomatic incident.

(NB: Other outcomes are possible.)

Example: *... since the Second World War ended in 1939...*

Problem: Did the author mean 'since the Second World War **began** in
1939' or 'since the Second World War ended in **1945** '. It might make a
difference.

**Example: *... the maximum permitted dose is 3 x 10 mg tablets or 300
mg per day***

Problem: Is the maximum dose 30 mg or 300 mg? It is essential to find out,
and to get the original corrected too, or someone may suffer an overdose.

What do the theorists have to say about this problem? Or indeed about translators' visibility in general?

AC

On mistakes in the original, modern empirical scholars would probably say:
let's study what professional translators do, and see how their decisions are
received by their clients and readers... (Are you still looking for advice...?)
Well, a [sic], or translator's note, or silent correction, or correction after consultation with the client – these are surely all standard solutions, and (except
silent correction) they all make the translator more visible to client and reader.

Some scholars might use the term **transediting** (coined by Stetting 1989)
to describe the strategy of correcting the source text in a covert way, with or
without consultation with the author. 'Doing nothing' might be called a literal translation strategy. Footnotes and [sic]s would be variants of a strategy
of addition. (We'll have more to say about strategies later, in Chapter 5.)

What the theorists have to say about visibility itself might not actually
seem very helpful in practice, at least at the kind of wordface where your
team are digging. Much of the discussion has been rather philosophical,
accepting translator invisibility as an unfortunate fact and looking for explanations. For example, a 1996 book by Douglas Robinson (appropriately called
Translation and Taboo) looks at the way translations and translators have
been traditionally banished to the periphery of social discourse and thus been
made invisible. Some ancient mystery cults actually banned translation. Recall the authorities' resistance to the first attempts to translate the Bible into a
vernacular language: translators were burned at the stake... Translations
and translators were 'taboo'. The deep-felt human awe of the sacred is some-

how bound up with this: to translate a holy text was to meddle with the sacred, and hence both mysterious and dangerous, not something to be talked about openly.

Lawrence Venuti has taken another approach to a similar conclusion. His book *The Translator's Invisibility* (1995b) deplores the way in which what he calls the **fluency ideal** has so dominated the Anglo-American translation tradition (he is talking about literary translation). This ideal entails the invisibility of the translator, as we have been discussing above. In order that translators should be more visible, Venuti therefore argues that, at least in the translation of literature, translators should resist the temptation to produce fluent target language, because this deceives readers into thinking that the text is in fact an original, not a translation. This fluent translation strategy denies the translators the right to be visible, and it also denies the source culture, the Other, the right to appear as something Different. Instead, Venuti suggests that, for certain text types, a *resistant* way of translating is thus more ethical – both with regard to the translator and with regard to the source culture. If you translate literature 'resistantly', you exploit more marked, unusual forms of the target language grammar and style; you might use archaisms or mix registers; and you might allow something of the original text to shine through the translation, as a kind of deliberate interference. Anyone reading such a translation would be aware that it was indeed a translation, that the original text was at home in a different culture.

You might also remember the postmodern image of the translator's carnival that I mentioned in our previous chapter: if the author is 'dead', let the translator wear the crown and thus be visible – until the translator fades away in turn and the reader takes over.

Ideas such as these may not seem so relevant to professionals working with other kinds of texts...?

EW

No, not at all relevant. Try explaining to readers who complain about Eurospeak and incomprehensible EU brochures that 'this is a resistant translation that allows the original to shine through'... you won't get very far. Ditto with your sobbing child, trying to understand the instructions for his computer game made in Japan.

You can see why so many translators think that theorists are a little out of touch with our day-to-day problems ...

AC

Actually, modern translation studies has done quite a bit to put translators on the map, I think. Historical studies have brought translators (usually literary, granted) into the limelight, and feminist scholars have discovered long-lost women translators (see von Flotow 1997). Cultural studies have shown the influence of translations on cultural development and cultural identity. There is a fascinating history of translating and interpreting (Delisle and Woodsworth 1995) that looks at the achievements of individual translators and interpreters through history. There is even polemical work (e.g. by Venuti 1995a) that studies translator's copyright and argues for the wider acceptance in law of the notion of dual authorship. Never before have there been so many departments of translator training in universities throughout the world. And there are dozens of professional associations that have helped to raise the visibility and impact of translators in society. Sociologically and institutionally, surely, translators in general have never had it so good.

EW

Yes. The jury may still be out on the usefulness of translation theory, but academics have certainly contributed to the visibility of the translation profession by providing practical training at university level. One of the people we have to thank for this, according to the Routledge *Encyclopedia of Translation Studies*, is the Polish poet Julian Tuwim (1894-1953). I quote:

> Tuwim's well-known essay *Traduttore – traditore,* published in 1950, castigated incompetent translators and put forward a proposal for organizing regular diploma courses for translators. Tuwim suggested that candidates should pass a series of examinations on language, stylistics and culture; only those who successfully completed the course would then be allowed to publish their work. (Tabakowska 1998:523)

Many others have contributed to making practical translation a respectable academic subject, and there has been a boom in undergraduate and postgraduate courses since the 1960s. Whatever one thinks of the courses – most of which seem to teach both translation and interpreting, on the sensible grounds that students only find out which suits them best by doing it – they have had a huge impact on the profession.

AC

If we think of the different ways in which an academic discipline makes progress, we can distinguish at least between internal and external progress. Internal progress is assessed in terms of scientific progress towards a theory, number of discovered facts and/or fruitful hypotheses, degree of increased understanding, etc., depending partly on what sort of discipline you have (remember our discussion in the first chapter). External progress, on the other hand, is reflected by the discipline's institutional development, its social visibility, and it is this that you are referring to with your reference to Tuwim.

In this respect, I agree entirely with your point. When translating/interpreting became a profession, something that not just anyone could do, something that needed special training – then it certainly gained in visibility and status. The next phase has only taken place in the past two or three decades: this training has achieved academic status, as something that is explicitly taught at universities or other university-level institutions. With this recognition have come academic posts, academic journals, scholarly conferences, etc. During the past ten years or so Translation Studies has come of age as a recognized academic discipline (or 'interdiscipline', as some prefer to say), although there is still quite some debate on what kind of discipline it is, as we discussed earlier. Specialized publications abound. There has appeared a *Dictionary of Translation Studies* (Shuttleworth and Cowie 1997), and an English-language one-volume *Encyclopedia of Translation Studies* (Baker 1998). A multi-volume De Gruyter encyclopedia is under preparation, with entries in English, German and French. And there is the *Handbuch Translation* in German (Snell-Hornby *et al.* 1998). I could go on...

So academic visibility has been spreading, and a good deal of external progress has been made. As for internal progress, well, opinions are divided. Some would claim that theoretical progress has been thin, that the wheel has been re-invented many times over. Others would argue that much has been discovered and made explicit that was previously only suspected, or not even suspected at all.

The visibility of the profession has surely also been enhanced by the founding of many scholarly and professional associations. On the scholarly side, we have associations like EST, the European Society for Translation Studies (http://est.utu.fi), which organizes a conference every three years and seeks to promote research into translation and interpreting.

EW

Yes, there are several professional associations, too: the grey-haired granny of them all is FIT (Fédération Internationale des Traducteurs), founded in 1953 and now acting as an umbrella organization for translators' and interpreters' associations throughout the world. It aims to encourage worldwide contacts and to promote professional status and standards. FIT has secured UN and UNESCO recognition, and contributed to the UNESCO Recommendation on the Protection and Improvement of the Legal and Social Status of Translations and Translators, adopted in Nairobi in 1976. It organizes congresses and symposia, and has sponsored projects such as the Delisle and Woodsworth's (1995) *Translators through History* that you mentioned. FIT's member associations include national bodies such as the well-established ITI (Institute of Translation and Interpreting) in Britain, and it maintains links with the interpreters' professional association AIIC (Association Internationale des Interprètes de Conférence).

In AIIC, the interpreters have an ally more muscular than any association representing translators. Perhaps because interpreting is the more visible profession? AIIC imposes stringent entry standards, works with universities to secure the right kind of training for interpreters, and has played an active part in negotiating pay and working conditions for its members: so much so that it is valued, respected, and in some cases feared, by the employers.

Yet most of the members of these professional associations are freelancers; in-house staff don't usually bother to join, perhaps because they get the social support and job security they need from being part of an in-house team. Perhaps too, because the national associations hold conferences and other events in their own country, and large numbers of in-house translators and interpreters are – almost by definition – employed outside their home country. Whatever the reasons for this reluctance to join, I think in-house staff are missing an opportunity to build solidarity between translators of all kinds and raise our collective profile. Too much fragmentation into factions will not help us as a profession.

It must also be admitted that membership of an association is not necessarily a guarantee of translation quality, just as having a translation diploma or degree does not guarantee that the holder is a skilled translator. If it did, employers would not need to hold their own entrance examinations or provide in-house training.

It might be mutually beneficial if at least part of the academic discipline of translation studies could be devoted to research on the effectiveness of translator training and performance standards. Topics could include: how best to pre-select and examine would-be translators; surveys of past students to see how many make it as professionals; contacting successful graduates and employers for feedback and practical input to improve university courses...

Two relevant initiatives that I know of (because they have contacted my organization, as an employer) are CIUTI and POSI:

* CIUTI (Conférence Internationale des Instituts Universitaires de Traducteurs et Interprètes) is an alliance of universities and training institutes that has attempted to harmonize course syllabuses and promote vocational standards;
* POSI (Praxisorientierte Studieninhalte) is an attempt by a group of European universities to liaise with experienced translators to provide, as the name suggests, practice-oriented study content.

A recent arrival on the translation scene is LISA, the Localization Industry Standards Association. This rather chic and glossy newcomer was formed to promote standards in software translation, project management and product information adapted to national markets. It is a commercial fact that international sales are affected by the availability of documentation and manuals in the right language: not everyone understands American English, and an incompetent translation into Dutch, Japanese or whatever can affect the company's credibility, however excellent the product.

The word 'standards' seems to be cropping up more and more here, as an adjunct of visibility. Isn't this inevitable?

AC

Standards, yes. An interesting theoretical point here is that people's concepts of translation seem inevitably bound up with their concepts of a *good* translation. A translation that is not a good one is scarcely worth having – scarcely seems to be recognized as a translation at all, in fact. Translations that are visible because they are so bad are, of course, regrettably common, but they are not recognized as professional products. They are not good examples of the concept 'translation' but dubious, borderline cases.

In order to promote standards, I agree, translators must themselves be visible socially and institutionally. There is some research on selecting translator trainees and on following up their professional success, but nowhere near enough. One problem is that just about anyone with some bilingual skills can set themselves up as 'a translator', advertise, find some translation work and produce some translations – regardless of how good they are, how much professional training they have had, etc. Compare the situation for doctors or engineers – as you said earlier. The professional status of translators is still so vague, so unprotected, that there are no adequate formal criteria separating competent professionals from incompetent amateurs: both groups can call themselves translators. What we need is a much stronger international accreditation system, such as the AIIC one for interpreters.

I think the key concept here is that of linking. If competent professional translators worldwide could link hands and establish a proper international standard, and if translator training in different countries could be harmonized to the extent of mutual recognition, translators would be much more visible as a profession and standards could more easily be maintained. Perhaps some kind of equivalent of the ISO or DIN quality assurance standards (see Chapter 6) could be developed, applicable to individual translators rather than translation companies as at present. This kind of cooperation could only strengthen the profession.

In another sense too, linking is the key to a translator's visibility. At one point in his book *Consilience* (1998: 121), the biologist E. O. Wilson discusses the role played by neural cells in the brain. They are apparently all connected to each other, constantly zapping messages back and forth across an incredibly complex network. This dynamic network seems to 'be' our sense of consciousness, of a self. In other words (Wilson here cites another biologist, S. J. Singer):

I link, therefore I am.

This is a wonderful motto for translators. Without links, the organ ceases to function.

At the social level, translators provide these links – in fact, they ARE these links. Each translator 'exists' by virtue of being a link: this is the fundamental justification of the profession, a justification that is ultimately both evolutionary and ethical. Evolutionary because of the survival value of making links, and ethical because of the necessity of connecting to something that is different from you, connecting to the Other.

Furthermore, the motto reminds us that the global community itself only exists as a co+mmunity by virtue of these links – like consciousness in the brain. Translators are thus like neural cells that have specialized in making particular kinds of links, and without these links the organ (the multilingual community) cannot live.

For quality of life, we therefore need quality of links...

4. What's it all for?

EW

'What's it for?' is a question translators should ask much more often, so they can translate accordingly. The following cautionary tale is based on an article by Chris Durban in the *ITI Bulletin* (1999: 30):

> With the liberalization of the EU's electricity market, the French utility Électricité de France (EDF) decided that it was time to establish their presence across Europe. So they placed a full-page ad in *The Financial Times*, *The Economist* and the *Wall Street Journal* (Europe). But the plan misfired... because of translation.
>
> The English text was a wobbly word-for-worder most charitably described as 'for information', and in any case woefully inadequate for a text-based full-page advertisement. Sample: EDF 'offers competitive energetic solutions' and 'is willing to accompany your development by following you on all of your sites in Europe and beyond'... 'in the electricity engineering, production, transmission and supply trades'. In case you wondered, 'its cash flow reaches 6.7 billion euros'.
>
> Who was to blame? EDF blamed their Paris-based advertising agency, which in turn blamed a translation agency. The translation agency said they had received no brief and had approached the job as they would have tackled translation of an in-house memo. They were unaware that the text had run unedited as advertising copy in the international press. Not surprisingly, the bad news triggered a run for cover: 'They didn't tell us what it was for. We provided a raw translation; it was up to them to have a copywriter check it.' Had the client wanted a ready-to-print (read: smooth) translation, they should have specified 'adaptation'...
>
> Yet the translation agency had not thought to ask the purpose of the text. So back up the chain the unwieldy translation lumbered, to be shot out into a black hole in space. Or unfortunately for the end client, into full-page displays in premium press vehicles across Europe.
>
> Impact on readers? 'EDF sound BIG, to be sure,' said one UK observer. 'But also arrogant, and anything but international. The text suggests that if you do contact them, you're likely to talk to French speakers with rudimentary English.'... An industry expert in Switzerland noted that the ad set up a subliminal message of a staunchly French identity 'directly at odds with the international image it was trying to achieve.' The whole exercise suggested a behemoth unaccustomed to putting itself in the place of its customers.
>
> For translation buyers, this sorry incident underscores the importance of forward planning, linking up with skilled suppliers prepared to stand by their work, and providing a brief for every single job. At the supplier end, it was a wake-up call for at least one agency: unless translators know where texts will appear and what clients want them to achieve, they cannot possibly produce a foreign-language text that works.

By the way, Chris Durban adds at the end of her article, the outlay on advertising space came to £104 855. The cost of translation was under £60.

From what you have said earlier (about skopos theory, for example, in Chapter 2) it seems that translation theory has something to say about this problem of matching (linking?) the product to the purpose. What?

AC

A cautionary tale, certainly, with a message for both clients and translators. Stupid of the clients not to specify what they wanted, and unprofessional of the translator not to find out. I wonder what kind of training the translator had? No one with a modern professional training would surely act like that, translating 'blind'. I am reminded of our discussion on chair theory – a client says 'I want a chair, please', and the carpenter says 'here you are, then', and then there is surprise when unspoken expectations do not match up to reality.

(Why are clients' instructions called a 'brief'? Because they are indeed brief – and usually not even the essentials are adequately covered...)

Yes, translation theory during the past couple of decades has taken a clearly functional line, in contrast to some of the older approaches that were based more on contrastive linguistics. By functional, I mean that these newer theories foreground the function of a translation, what it is supposed to be for. **Skopos theory** does this most explicitly, as I mentioned earlier: *skopos* means 'purpose' or 'aim' or 'goal', and skopos theory (in its simplest form) says just that the form of a translation is determined by its function – at least, this applies to ideal translations, translations as they should be. A bit like functionalism in architecture: remember the slogan 'form follows function'?

Scholars have probed into this idea of a functional theory in different ways, and done some conceptual analysis that you may, or may not, find useful. Some, such as Christiane Nord (1997), break down the notion of skopos into three separate components: intention, function, and effect. An **intention** is something in the mind of the sender of the message: the purpose that the sender wishes to achieve. In Nord's analysis, the **function** of a translation is a property of the translation itself, separate (in principle) from the sender's intention; the function is assigned to a translation by the recipient, who takes the translation to be a text functioning in a particular way, with a particular point. The **effect**, then, refers to what happens in the recipient's mind and/or behaviour after reading the translation. In your example, the client's intention was presumably to promote a particular image, let us say image A; the function of the text was assumed by the readers to be (partly) the promotion of a different image, B (the function thus represents the recipient's guess as to the sender's intention); the actual effect seems to have been the establishment of image C, which was in obvious conflict with image A. In ideal cases, and in good professional translation, intention, function and effect all coincide.

We could simplify this a bit and say that the skopos is the intended effect of the translation, but some people might say this just skates over the complexity of the issue. Intended by whom? Do the client's intentions always take precedence over anyone else's, such as the actual source-text writer's for instance, if that writer is someone different from the client? Can you even define intentions at all, in any more than a very rough way? Literary scholars have long warned us not to believe that we can have much access to an author's intentions. And what about the translator's own intentions? Postmodern scholars would want to give these a place, too (see Vieira 1994; Arrojo 1998).

Furthermore: effect on whom? On all readers? Just some readers? Just intended readers? Would this mean excluding some potential readers? Can you even predict who will read the translation? Effects at a given time only, or for all time? And surely effects are just as hard to pin down as intentions are? Lots of interesting problems here, say the theorists.

EW

Yes, they are right. But let's try to untangle the complexity a bit. It might be helpful, for the moment, to disregard the literary scholars, and especially the postmodern scholars with their esoteric concerns. To me, they all seem excessively concerned with the intentions of individuals – individual authors, individual translators. But non-literary texts don't necessarily 'belong' to an individual – as I think I've already said, they are often a collective effort, rarely an exercise in individual self-expression. They are different from literary texts because:

a) They are written for a purpose – to sell a product, explain a policy, give instructions for use, etc. The author's (and translator's) skills must be devoted to serving this purpose, not to expressing their own individuality.
b) They are not as perfectly written as literature, whose form is by definition final. In non-literary texts, it is legitimate to give the authors some help, by adapting the form to fit the function. Effects on readers are hard to pin down – harder than intentions – but that problem arises with all writing, with or without translation. Translation just adds another group of potential readers.

AC

Literary texts surely also have 'purposes' – albeit perhaps less specific ones than those you mention. But OK, let's focus on non-literary texts for the moment. Take the model presented by Juan Sager (1994), for example. Sager has specialized in the study of commercial translation, translation as an industrial practice. His analysis of the kind of thing we are talking about might be more relevant to your concerns.

For Sager, a message is a text plus a purpose, and a purpose is defined as a convergence of an intention (the sender's or writer's) and an expectation (the reader's). He recognizes that a given text can be read in different ways, by readers with different expectations, and that the resulting combinations of intention and expectation can give rise to different purposes. That is, one and the same text, written and/or sent with a given intention, can give rise to different effects on different readers, e.g. at different times or in different circumstances. From this point of view, communicating successfully means knowing something about the expectations of your readers/hearers, so that you can adjust the form of your message in such a way that the combination of your intention and your readers' expectations gives rise to the appropriate purpose.

Coming back to your example again, we could say that the clients failed to communicate successfully to the translation agency, and that the agency failed to transmit the intended message to the readers of the translation, because in both cases no account was taken of the other party's expectations. As the article you cited put it, it was like sending off a message into a black hole. Perhaps both clients and translators should be encouraged to use their imagination a bit more, to imagine the expectations of their intended and potential readers, to imagine the conditions under which their message will be received. This might help to ensure that it was received in the sense it was intended.

In fact, both the client and the translation agency in your example were acting rather solipsistically: neither seems to be aware that they were communicating to *someone else*, with different expectations; they were talking to themselves only. And this makes the problem an ethical one, doesn't it? How do you communicate to someone who is not yourself? But I digress...

EW

Here again, I think we could cut down the angst if we untangled things a bit. In the EDF story there were numerous breakdowns in communication, yes. Probably, as you say, because everyone failed to take account of the other party's expectations. But it might help if we made a clear distinction between two different stages of communication: Stage A – from client to translator, and Stage B – from translator to reader.

At Stage A, the clients (authors and commissioners of translations) need some way of telling the translator what the text is for (= briefing). At present, there is no commonly understood way of specifying the purpose and intended readership of a text. Instead, it is even argued:
* that it is the translator's duty to find out the purpose (you said yourself that it was 'unprofessional of the translator not to find out'); or
* that divining the author's intention is one of the marks of a skilled translator. Indeed, it might seem easy to work out the underlying intention of *Software Manual XJ750, Application for research grant, Conference paper on waste recycling*, etc. But is it? Are you translating the conference paper 'for publication' in the conference proceedings, on behalf of the author? Or are you translating it 'for information', for someone who has been advised to read the conference proceedings but doesn't understand the language they're written in? The words on the page don't tell the whole story – so, as with the EDF advertising copy, we need a more explicit brief.

At Stage B, where the translator has to communicate with the reader, the reader's expectations matter (naturally). This is a different problem from the briefing at Stage A, and calls for different solutions.

AC

At both your stages, one might argue that the key principle is simply that of **relevance** – yet another way to conceptualize this problem area. That is, at Stage A it is the client's job to give the translator the relevant information for the translation task, and at Stage B it is up to the translator to find the most relevant means of communicating the desired message.

One approach to translation studies actually makes relevance the kingpin of everything. The main contributor here has been Ernst-August Gutt (2000), whose background is that of a Bible translator. He argues that translation does not need a separate theory of its own, because it is covered by general communication theory – in particular, by the kind of communication theory known as relevance theory, which has become part of mainstream pragmatics nowadays. (By pragmatics, I mean the study of 'language in use', roughly speaking.)

The relevance theory of communication (including translation) claims that the guiding principle of communication (and therefore translation) is relevance: you say and/or write in such a way that your words are optimally relevant to your hearers/readers. This means roughly that what you say should have maximum **contextual effect** (benefit) and require minimum **processing effort** (cost). Strictly speaking, the benefit should be proportionate to the cost: the more benefit at less cost, the more relevant a message is. Really *big* messages tend to be very easy to process: will you marry me? Danger!

(Note how the value of clarity gets a pragmatic justification here! Clarity means easy processing, and hence a better cost-benefit ratio, and hence better relevance.)

In relevance theory, an effect is preliminarily defined as a cognitive change in the mind of the reader. This may not seem to get us very far, but the point becomes clearer when you realize that changes always occur in a context, not in a vacuum. Similarly, messages are understood in a context, and their reception cannot be analyzed or predicted without such a context. The importance of the theory, as I see it, is the way it takes into account the reader's expectations, the reader's situational context and cognitive experience, as factors that impinge upon the choices of the speaker/writer/translator. Because unless you know something about these expectations, etc., you cannot formulate your message in an optimally relevant way. You must be able to guess the context that your reader will bring to your text, in the light of which s/he will interpret it. Skopos theory and relevance theory thus seem to be looking at the same point from different angles. 'Be relevant to the purpose'. – Would that do as one of the guidelines you keep asking for?

EW

No, that's not the sort of guideline translators want. Too abstract. Interesting stuff, but we need a more explicit, concrete framework – a clear language in which we can talk about intentions, functions and effects to our clients, our readers, and our fellow translators. What I want is a way of defining intentions (maybe by creating a terminology to make them more explicit), classifying translation approaches in terms of text function, and maybe categorizing readerships too, in terms of expectations.

AC

Could you give me an example of what you WOULD consider a useful guideline?

EW

A useful guideline would be:

> 'Never translate blind. Get the client to brief you on the purpose and intended readership of the translation. Then translate accordingly'.

Useful adjuncts would be: a short and simple list of purposes (or *skopoi* if you insist); of readers; of translation types to suit the specified purpose and readership.

The list of purposes has to be clear enough for clients to understand it, and to see why it is in their interests to use it. Translators, too, need to understand why they should translate differently for different purposes. Surprisingly many translators will argue that a translator's duty is to translate *accurately* (not to make a silk purse out of a sow's ear) and *in full* (not just to give the gist). But sometimes a silk purse, or just the gist, is what the client needs.

Here's one list of translation purposes based on practice at the wordface. It may not be an exhaustive typology, but it would have prevented the EDF fiasco. This list is taken from *A Practical Guide for Translators* by Geoffrey Samuelsson-Brown (1993: 50). The author is a very experienced technical translator who runs his own translation company. He summarizes the common reasons for ordering a translation as follows:

Information
Publication
Advertising and marketing
Litigation
Text scanning and abstracting

I think this list – though excellent – could be improved slightly. Unfortunately, the all-important difference between translation for 'information' and translation for 'publication' is frequently misunderstood or denied, even by professional translators.

A translation for **information** (also known as 'inbound translation') is a translation intended for one user or a small group of users who need to know what the original text says and will probably discard the translation once they've found out. This type of translation calls for speed and a correct rendering of the information content; style and quality control are less important.

Translation for **publication** (or 'outbound translation') is a different animal. Here, the reputation of the author or an organisation will stand or fall on your translation. All work for publication should be revised or at least looked at by 'a second pair of eyes'. It may need to be presented in a special format or to follow special in-house style rules which are irrelevant in a translation for information.

Translating **promotional material** is yet another type of translation. Here, the persuasive effect on the reader is far more important than faithful reproduction of the original (which usually has a most unpersuasive effect). Translators have a duty to point out to clients that advertisements cannot simply be translated and have the same effect in another language. In any case, different countries have different marketing methods and this must be respected. Of the Top Ten Misconceptions about Translation (on the Internet, *passim*) the number one misconception is: 'That marketing copy that took a team of 20 people two months to put together can be translated overnight by one person and still retain the same impact as the original'.

With **legal translations,** especially those to be used as evidence in court, the translator carries great responsibility and quality control is essential.
Clients should be asked to make it clear whether legal translations are required as legal documents in their own right, or simply 'for information' (see above). In the latter case, translators are advised to add a statement along the following lines: "*Although due care and attention has been given to this translation, it should not be considered a legal document and the original language document takes precedence over this translation in any dispute over interpretation*".

Text scanning is partial translation. Sometime a client just needs the translator to read through the whole text and extract relevant information. Geoff Samuelsson-Brown (1993: 51) says, "a good example is an invitation to tender for a particular contract. The client may be able to decide as a result of your scanning whether the contract is worth bidding for". **Abstracting** means summarising the main information in a text and reproducing it (in translated form) in a fixed number of words.

With a few minor changes, the above list can be converted into a short and simple list of translation purposes. I think it's better to say 'For information, *not* for publication' just to ensure that a translation obtained for one purpose is not subsequently used for another. And I would change 'Litigation' to 'For use as a legal document' in order to include contracts and other binding documents that will have legal force independently of the original. Let's hope that actual litigation can be avoided!

A short and simple list of translation purposes

For information, not for publication
For publication
For advertising and marketing
For use as a legal document
For text scanning and abstracting

This classification is much better than nothing. Of course it has some limitations – for example, the purpose 'for publication' is a very wide field and can range from an academic treatise to a cartoon strip. And nowadays 'for publication' must include websites and CD-ROMs as well as traditional paper publications, some of which may have promotional purposes too, so the translations are also 'for advertising and marketing'. Despite these criticisms, I feel that a simple list of purposes would improve communication between translators and their clients and should ideally be included in some kind of international translation standard (as I'll explain in Chapter 6, this hasn't happened yet). What do you think of the classification?

AC

Your list of purposes looks useful for non-literary texts. Literary translation would presumably come under 'for publication'. 'Purposes' sound a bit more down to earth than 'functions' or 'skopoi'. Your interpretation of 'for publication' evidently excludes advertising and marketing, which might be a debatable point, but I think it is a good idea to distinguish this kind of overtly persuasive purpose somehow. In the theoretical literature classifications of this kind have tended to start at a very abstract level, with functions of language in general. One classical starting point is Bühler's model (used in Reiss 2000 and Reiss and Vermeer 1984), according to which language has three basic functions:

* to refer to something (the **referential** or **informative** function, oriented towards the subject matter);
* to persuade, instruct, or otherwise get someone to do something (oriented towards the receiver; Reiss calls texts with this function **operational texts**);
* to express the speaker's feelings and ideas (**expressive** function, oriented towards the speaker).

In any given use of language, these are often all present, of course; but we can usually say which is the most dominant one, for instance in a particular part of a text. Advertising and marketing texts would be mostly receiver-oriented; texts 'for information' would be classified as having a referential function. Other scholars have proposed more complex classifications, including the **aesthetic** or **poetic** function, the **phatic** function (i.e. the goal of simply establishing or maintaining contact), and even the **metalinguistic** function (to say something about language itself).

EW

This is not the sort of terminology we can use for communicating with clients ('Excuse me, but does this report have a phatic or a referential function?') but that is not what it is intended for, of course. It would not be realistic to expect to use the same jargon for quasi-commercial interactions with our clients, for conversations between translators, and in academic theory. All the same, I think Bühler's model could possibly be built into some of the questions we need to ask at the briefing stage:

What was it written for?
(to inform? to persuade? to express the author's feelings or ideas?)

Who was it written for?
(insiders? specialists? general public?)

What is it being translated for?
(to inform? to persuade? to express the author's ideas?)

Who is it being translated for?
(insiders? specialists? general public?)

AC

These questions are of course addressed in any functional description of the translation process – the ideal process, anyway. I'll take Sager's (1994) model as an example. Your Stage A (briefing) is what Sager calls the **specification** phase, which is then followed by what he calls the **preparation** and **translation** phases (incorporating your Stage B), and then the **evaluation/revision** phase.

Sager analyses the components of the specification phase from the point of view of the translator rather than that of the client: the following questions and points represent what the translator has to know before proceeding to later phases. (I would add: translators must either know these things already, e.g. in the case of a routine text, or find them out from the client. Conversely, the client should have to provide this information, either automatically or on request.)

1. Identifying the source language document
What kind of document is it? What is its text type and general topic?

2. Identifying the intention
Who is the document for?
And: *What* is the document for? Should the translation have a different intention from that of the source text (which will require some adaptation)?

3. Interpreting the specifications
What type of document should the translation be? (Not necessarily the same type as the source text.)
What is the expected reaction of the recipient?
What information can be presupposed, i.e. what can we assume that the recipient already knows?

> Other relevant situational factors here are those of time (the speed-quality
> ratio required), cost, and direction (incoming or outgoing, with respect to
> an organization such as yours).
>
> 4. Cursory reading
> What is the document about?

You might say this is all common sense – but so it should be, I guess. It is one
way of trying to make explicit the various factors involved, most of which
you yourself mentioned earlier.

Similar analyses are proposed by other scholars, with different
terminologies and classifications, but basically covering the same ground.
Christiane Nord's (1997) model, for instance, lists a number of **extratextual**
factors (such as sender, intention, time, function, medium) and **intratextual**
factors (including presuppositions, subject matter, text composition). She fo-
cuses on how a close analysis of the source text can reveal much of the kind
of information we are discussing here; the client's responsibility to provide it
is not highlighted, nor is the importance of consultation between the translator and the client. Indeed, Nord points out that clients are often unable to give
precise instructions because they are ignorant of the complexity of the translation process. In my view, it would often be quicker to ask the client directly
than trying to infer information from a detailed analysis of the source text.

EW

Yes, you're right. Of course many of us here at the wordface would sympa-
thize with Christiane Nord's view "that clients are often unable to give precise
instructions because they are ignorant of the complexity of the translation
process". But let's be realistic: our aim is to get a brief so we can deliver the
right product, not to instruct them about the translation process. When I order
a coffee, I don't need to know about the internal workings of the espresso
machine. But I will have to specify whether I want large, small, black, white,
decaf... (Actually it is astoundingly complex to order a coffee these days.) As
you say, it is quicker to ask the client directly than to try to infer information
from a detailed analysis of the source text. Especially when you are in an
international organization like the European Commission, where the same
text has to be translated into several languages. So you may have as many
as ten translators desperately trying to infer things that one person could
have found out by lifting the telephone and asking the right questions. At
least we are able to contact our clients – unlike freelance translators, who
may be at the end of a Chinese-whispers chain of agencies, subcontractors
and intermediaries. Not being able to contact the author/client is a major problem for translators.

The relation between the reader, the client and the author can vary. These are the possible scenarios:

---

1. CLIENTS WHO ARE AUTHORS
These may be either:
(a) clients who have written the text in their mother tongue, and are having it translated so others can understand;
or
(b) clients who have written the text in a foreign language and are having it translated into their mother tongue (yes, they do exist – and can be the most difficult type of client).

2. CLIENTS WHO ARE MIDDLEMEN
between the reader(s) and the author. These are often translation agencies or secretaries who have been instructed to 'get this translated!'.
Here we have the full range:
from
(a) good clients who know the purpose of the translation and understand both the original and the target languages;
to
(z) bad clients who know nothing (purpose or language) and don't care. Except perhaps about the deadline and the fee (as low as possible).

3. CLIENTS WHO ARE READERS
These clients need the translation because they don't understand the source language. They may be either:
(a) the sole reader;
or
(b) one of many potential readers.

So you can see that 'client' is a rather dangerous blanket term. But now we've worked out what questions we should be asking our various clients, and the replies they might give, we should look at the product range we can provide to meet the purposes specified. In other words, translation types...

AC

Classifications of translation types have traditionally been binary ones. Perhaps the oldest is literal vs. free translation, going back to the text-type difference between sacred texts (to be translated literally, for fear of changing the Word of God) and literary texts (that could be translated more freely). Contemporary scholars have proposed other binary classifications. Peter Newmark (1981), for instance, speaks of semantic translation and communicative translation. **Semantic translation** is appropriate for any text whose form has a high status in the source culture, such as philosophical and literary texts as well as sacred texts; it respects the form of the original, and keeps as close as possible to the exact meaning. **Communicative translation** is freer, more reader-friendly, more natural target language. Newmark's illustrative examples include the following one:

Source text: *Défense de marcher sur le gazon.*
Semantic translation: *Walking on the turf is forbidden. | It is forbidden to walk on the turf.*
(Function: to show how this is said in French.)
Communicative translation: *Keep off the grass.*
(Function: to serve as a notice for English speakers.)

When you read a semantic translation, you probably realize at once that it is indeed a translation (and/or perhaps written by a non-native speaker). Some translations are indeed intended by the translator and the client to be recognized in this way: for instance a translation of legislation in the source culture, for the information of a lawyer in the target culture); even literature can be translated in this way. Juliane House (1997) calls these **overt** translations, in contrast to **covert** ones, which are not supposed to be recognized as translations. In other words, covert translations are the kind that are written in very fluent, natural target language, to give the impression that they are in fact not translations at all. Overt translations, on the other hand, are written in a more marked style, preserving indicators that tie the text to its original culture. Covert translations are appropriate for certain purposes, overt ones for others.

The same kind of distinction is also made by Christiane Nord (1997), but in different terms: she opposes **documentary** translation and **instrumental** translation. A documentary translation is one that acts openly as a document referring to a text in another language – such as the translation of an exam certificate or work reference. An instrumental translation functions as an 'instrument' in its own right, without links to a source text: examples would include advertisements, tourist brochures (in theory!), washing-machine instructions, and so on.

EW

Is the distinction between overt and covert translations really the same as the distinction between documentary and instrumental ones? If so, it seems confusing to keep inventing new terms for the same thing.

AC

Agreed. But there is more... Recent suggestions concerning translation typology have been rather more complex, focussing less on defining types than on analyzing the criteria that seem to be relevant for setting up classifications in the first place. Here are some of the criteria that have been proposed:

* Is the intended function of the translation the same as or different from the function of the original?;

* Is all the content translated, or only some of it? (If only some, the result might be a kind of translation known as **gist** translation. Subtitling is another kind of translation that typically has a reduced content.);
* Is the form of the translation the same as that of the original? At what level: morpheme, word, phrase, sentence, paragraph, layout, something else? (Think of dubbing, for instance, which tries to approximate to the same lip movements. Or linguistic/philological glosses, in academic texts, which try to match the word or morpheme structure of the original.);
* Is the style of the translation 'the same' as that of the original (e.g. the formality level, or the relation to everyday spoken language)?;
* Does the translation correct (in some way) any factual errors in the original?;
* What is the relative status of the source and target texts? Is the original thrown away, for instance, as soon as the translation is ready? Do both texts remain in parallel? Or does the translation have a clearly secondary status (e.g. in law)?;
* How natural is the language of the translation? Native but clumsy? Native but unusual? Intelligible but not entirely grammatical? (Are the readers supposed to be aware that it is a translation?);
* Is the translation localized to target culture conditions?;
* Is the translation matched to a house style?;
* Is the translation done by a native speaker of the target language?;
* Are there special constraints of space or time?;
* Does the translation involve a change of medium (e.g. spoken to written)?

EW

Help! This is going too far. And it sounds suspiciously like a typology for classifying completed translations after the event, not a way of helping translators to decide how to tackle a new job...

AC

Yes, that's true. These distinctions have been set up mainly to help descriptive scholars to analyze types of already-existing translations, in order to make generalizations about typical features of some type of translation. If we work out all the possible combinations of these, we will end up with a very complex typology indeed! This might be theoretically interesting, but would be of little practical value. I guess what you would like would be a set of basic common types that would be less complex than this, but more detailed than the binary ones I mentioned earlier.

Gouadec (1990), also using some of the above criteria, proposes seven translation types:

Keyword translation (translating the keywords only);
Selective translation (not all the content);
Abstract translation (just producing a summary);
Diagrammatic translation (giving the sense of the original in the form of a
diagram, i.e. changing the medium);
Translation with reconstructions (all the content, but in a very free form);
Absolute translation (warts and all, nothing corrected);
Sight translation (written to spoken).

Other isolated suggestions by other scholars include these (from Shuttleworth
and Cowie 1997):

Thick translation
    (with mountains of explications and footnotes; similar to Ethnographic
    translation and exegetic translation);
Cultural translation
    (heavily adapted to the target culture);
Horizontal translation
    (between languages and cultures of roughly equal status; compare Ver-
    tical translation, between a vernacular and a high-prestige language
    such as Latin, in the Middle Ages);
Integral translation
    (with no omissions or additions above the sentence level);
Interlinear translation
    (with the source text present alongside the translation);
Intralingual translation
    (rewriting within the same language);
Polemical translation
    (in which the translator deliberately and openly diverges from the au-
    thor's intention, or from the interpretation of another translator);
Radical translation
    (in philosophy, translation from a language no one has translated out of
    before, so the translator is never quite sure what anything means...);
and then all the terms denoting various ways of translating poetry.

With all this in mind, perhaps you can suggest the kind of typology that
you would find useful?

EW

Phew. There seems to be some confusion between translation purposes, text
types and translation types. But let's concentrate on translation types. In practice, the full range of translation types stretches from the very basic
'Is-it-rat-poison?' to the top-of-the-range 'Ted-Hughes', which are not normally

supplied by professional non-fiction translators. But there are several inter-mediate types, which are normally supplied.

Bottom of the range, not normally supplied by professional translators

* **word-for-word translation** Basic product, helps the tourist in the Greek super-market to tell if that white powder is sugar, salt, detergent or rat poison.

Translation types most commonly supplied

* **straight translation**
Nothing corrected or adapted – same as Gouadec's 'absolute' translation.

* **tidied translation**
Author's mistakes corrected, but the translation is not adapted. This is probably the standard default type but doesn't seem to be mentioned by the theorists?

* **naturalized translation**
Author's mistakes corrected, form and style of translation adapted so that it feels like an original text in the target culture. Which may not be a national culture, but a global one. In which case we could speak of 'internationalized' translation. This may be similar to 'cultural translation, or Gouadec's 'translation with reconstruc-tions' or Nord's 'instrumental' translation.

* **reduced translation**
Just the basic information or 'message' is translated – could be the same as Gouadec's 'keyword', 'selective' or 'abstract' translation.

Top of the range

* **artistic translation**
Produced by Ted Hughes *et al.*

There are several other recognizable but less common translation types in your list: Gouadec's 'sight translation' is one I recognize – also called 'oral translation', and we do it occasionally, but not nearly as often as we did in the classroom all those years ago. Some people would say that machine transla-tion and preprocessed translation (with a translation memory) are separate types, but I would not agree – they are translation methods, not types.

Among the other types you mentioned, some useful concepts are *polemi-cal* translation – to be avoided at all costs in most professional contexts ('Don't recruit him, his translations are far too polemical!') – and *intralingual* transla-tion or rewriting within the same language. This is on the increase, and it is done for various reasons: editing of badly written originals prior to translation, rewriting for a different audience (e.g. producing the simplified 'Peter and Jane' version of a technical report for politicians), and pre-editing for machine translation. So, if we try to match the most common purposes with most com-mon translation types:

Purpose	Translation type
For information, not for publication	Straight (if author's mistakes must be reproduced) Tidied (if author's mistakes are to be corrected)
For publication	Naturalized (for national audience) Internationalized (for international audience)
For advertising and marketing	Naturalized or even artistic
For use as a legal document	Straight (if the text is to be used as evidence) Tidied (with permission, if the text is a contract or other legal act)
For text scanning and abstracting	Reduced

AC

That's a nice minimal set of useful translation types for non-literary texts. The 'tidied' type does not really appear as a distinct kind of translation in the theoretical literature, true, but the idea of source-text editing is of course familiar. Many writers have commented on this, and we also touched on it ourselves in Chapter 3.

EW

Once translators have decided on the most appropriate translation type, they may also want to adapt the style, register or 'technicality' of the translation to the needs of the probable readers. For example, take a medical report written by a foreign doctor for someone who falls ill while on holiday abroad. It might have to be translated 'for information' (or, if you're unlucky, 'for use as a legal document'). The translation type would be 'straight' or 'tidied', depending on the doctor's handwriting, etc. A report full of medical jargon would need to be translated in one way for a doctor in the patient's home country, but in another way for the patient, using simpler language or adding translator's notes that would be unnecessary or even irritating for a doctor. So in addition to purpose and translation type, the target readers have to be brought into the equation too. Is there any recognized way of classifying readers?

AC

As for readers, here again, we can offer some general classifications, but I wonder how useful you will find them. Here are a few examples.

* *Homocultural* vs *heterocultural*: to what extent do the readers form a homogeneous group? A homogeneous audience might expect more in-group language, technical terms; for a heterogeneous audience a more popular style might be appropriate. The most heterogeneous readership would be 'the general public'; on the other hand, a research report to be published in a scientific journal would have a more homogeneous readership.
* *Native* or *non-native* speakers (of the target language)? If the assumed

readers include non-native speakers (one kind of heterogeneity), it might not be a good idea to use lots of colourful contemporary idioms or unusual words or very complex structures. This seems particularly important for translating into English, as a global language.

* *Cultural distance* between source and target cultures: the more the distance, the greater the need may be for adaptation, explanation, expansions, footnotes, and so on.

* The *vertical translation* dimension: this refers to the possible difference in cultural prestige between the source and target cultures. Historical studies show that translators who work from a 'higher' or 'bigger' or 'dominating' culture into a 'lower' one tend to use different strategies compared to those used by translators working from a 'lower' into a 'higher' culture. There seem to be differences, for instance, in the way 'local colour' is accepted in translations from big or small cultures. Whether this *should* be the case is a different matter. But it does seem to make a difference whether you are 'translating down' or 'translating up'.

* *Addressees vs. receivers* (or recipients). An 'addressee' is an intended or implied reader, as imagined by the client or the translator (one hopes that client and translator have the same kinds of addressee in mind). A 'receiver' is a real reader, who actually does read the text: the set of receivers ideally includes the set of addressees, but may well be much larger. See also the following dimension.

* The *participation* dimension: Anthony Pym (1992a) has suggested there are three kinds of text receiver. A **participative** receiver is one to whom a text is explicitly addressed, an assumed or intended reader (e.g. people reading a job advertisement who might really think of applying). An **observational** reader is someone who understands a given text even though they know it is not addressed to them; they 'overhear' the text (readers of the job ad who are not even thinking of changing their job or who are clearly not qualified to apply). And an **excluded** reader is unable to receive the message (at all, or in part), because the language is unfamiliar, the content too difficult, or whatever. This dimension brings in an interesting ethical aspect: in many cases, it might be ethically appropriate to translate in such a way that the group of excluded readers is as small as possible.

Theoretical contributions to these matters, as I said, have tended to start with such rather abstract distinctions, and you might say that they are rather far removed from your wordface. But remember that theorists are trying to construct a general conceptual map of the whole business. A bit like architects starting with concepts like mass, gravity, light, dimension, form and so on.

If we now proceed downwards on the way to your guidelines, the next level is probably that of translation types (compare: basic types of building).

And then, further down still, we might find more specific strategic recommendations for solving particular problem types (how to choose the right concrete, how to design adequate supporting pillars, and so on).

EW

(Is that what architects really do? Start with abstract concepts like mass, gravity, light? That explains a lot...)

The classifications of readers look quite useful, actually. I'm not sure about bigger or dominating cultures being 'higher' – sounds dubious. Is a hamburger 'higher' than a pizza? But I like the 'participation dimension' and the idea of three kinds of text receiver (participative, observational and excluded) because it reflects readers' attitudes.

Here's a similar unofficial classification of readers that some colleagues of mine have suggested, reflecting attitudes and cultural distance:

* in-house readers ('family');
* informed outsiders ('friends');
* public ('foreigners'), divided into individual, specialist and general readers.

'Family' means in-house colleagues, who don't mind exclusive jargon (may even prefer it). 'Friends' are outside the organization, but kindly disposed to it, willing to make a few concessions. 'Foreigners' are outsiders who may be sceptical, even hostile, and need to be addressed differently.

Readers' levels of interest and knowledge will always vary. I have tried to argue that writing – and translation – should be tailored to the purpose and the readers. If that is the case, then any attempt to produce a single all-inclusive translation – one that will suit every reader – is doomed to failure. Forget all those tedious debates about literal versus free translation, etc. There is a place for both of them, and several other types, depending on the purpose, depending on the readers.

'*What's it all for?* – the title of this chapter – is a wider question too. In our discussion of functions, purposes, translation types and readers we have tried to suggest ways of illuminating the windowless cell in which many translators feel trapped, and to shine some light into another black box – the one to which clients are so often consigned. Some of the suggestions we have made here, and the uncertainties they may generate, will doubtless displease those purists who argue that translators should 'just translate'. Some of my fellow translators would be shocked by my suggestion that the same text should be translated differently depending on the needs of the reader (the medical report translated in one way for a doctor and in another for a patient). But what's the point of a translation if it doesn't speak to people in their language? If it doesn't help them to understand? That is 'what it's all for' – to mediate, to convey a message, to provide a service. Translators who understand the need for a differentiated service, and develop the versatility to provide it, will have more satisfied customers and more job satisfaction. But it is not easy to ask one's clients (and oneself) all these questions. The easy option is to stay in the windowless cell and 'just translate'.

5. How do I get there?

AC

Research on translation strategies is a popular area these days. We start by looking at the translating process as a form of problem-solving. (This kind of research has actually helped to move the theoretical focus from the product – analyzing or criticizing translations – to the process, carried out by real people.) Standard definitions tend to say that a *problem* is an incompatibility between ends and means: we have an end in view, but we don't know (immediately) how to get there from where we are now. How do we get from our present state to the desired state? The term *strategy* is then used to describe well-established procedures, proven methods of solving particular kinds of problems and reaching the desired goal. Many of the strategies studied seem to be received ideas in the professional translator community: that is why we try to teach them to students.

Think of a carpenter making, say, a bookcase. At one point, s/he has to make a particular kind of joint. How should s/he do it? An experienced professional will presumably know at once what tool to use, how to make the necessary cuts, what glue is best, etc. Translation strategies are like conceptual tools in a translator's toolkit.

Different kinds of strategies are used for different kinds of problems.

We might divide our problem types as follows:

Search problems? $\Rightarrow$ Search strategies
Blockage problems? $\Rightarrow$ Creativity strategies
Text problems? $\Rightarrow$ Textual strategies

Search problems: how to find a specific term, where to look on the Internet, whom to telephone... For these, we need search strategies: the kind of thing taught in professional translation courses: how to use dictionaries, how to find and use parallel texts (untranslated, target-language texts of the same kind as the translation you are working on), how to find and use term banks, and so on.

Blockage problems: what do you do when you get stuck, when the brain no longer seems to flow? Popular creativity strategies include solutions like going for a walk, having another coffee, asking a colleague, listening to jazz or Mozart, sleeping on it, thinking about something else for a bit, daydreaming, and moving on a different bit of the text. These do not seem to be actually taught much, but they do get talked about over coffee.

> *Text problems*: how to process a particular bit of source text, how to come up with more alternative versions to choose from; how to translate metaphors, dialect, allusions, inversion structures, rhetorical questions; when to use loanwords, footnotes, neologisms? The textual strategies that professionals use for solving problems like these have been much studied, much more than the other two types above.

EW

Solving translation problems may look as easy and intuitive as picking up the right tool, but it doesn't always feel that way. Translation is difficult, and we professionals are plagued by self-doubt. If you ask a translator why s/he translated X as A instead of B, s/he is quite likely to say 'Because I didn't think of B. Good idea, thanks'.

AC

As you may have noticed, academics like making distinctions. We also like inventing new labels for approximately the same thing. Research on translation strategies is no exception, so here goes... I'll start with the textual ones, as they have been studied most.

First, we can distinguish between **global** and **local** textual strategies. Global strategies apply to the whole text, and they are usually decisions that the translator makes before starting to translate. Examples:

* *Adaptation*: the whole text needs to be adapted to the target culture, and therefore nothing should be left that links it specifically to the source culture, perhaps not even proper names. (This is frequently used in the translation of children's literature; also when translating advertisements.)
* *Foreignization*: the text needs to retain its foreignness, for aesthetic or cultural reasons, so target language fluency is not a priority. (This is often used in the translation of literature.)

EW

This two-way choice between foreignizing and adapting (domesticating?) is a bit simplistic, I think. Surely there are more than two options, and the global strategy must take account of the text purpose and intended readership as discussed above?

Presumably you would agree that translators may have to adopt other global strategies depending on the purpose of the document and the intended readership, e.g.

* *simplifying* = translating technical or specialized terms using everyday language (e.g. an EU text for the man in the street, farmer in the field, etc.);
* *explaining* = expanding acronyms and explaining unfamiliar concepts, maybe with footnotes or translators' notes (e.g. translating a degree certificate);
* *condensing* = summarizing the main message (for readers in a hurry);
* *straight translation* = translating in order to show what the original text says, without concessions (e.g. translating exam answers or research proposals – texts that will be used to assess the authors).

AC

Yes, we need more than a two-way choice of global strategy. **Local strategies**, on the other hand, apply to particular segments of the text. You might prefer to think of them as **tactics**, actually. Other terms that some people prefer are **procedures**, **methods**, **shifts** or **changes**.

Shifts and **changes** highlight the fact that the textual strategies we are talking about are ways of altering various linguistic aspects of the source text as we construct the translation. The first scholars who got interested in this kind of thing were in fact theoretical and applied linguists, who saw translation as a kind of recoding (recall our earlier chapter). They compared source and target texts, did a contrastive analysis, and ended up with a typology of linguistic changes. So we find results such as: where French tends to use an abstract noun, English tends to use a concrete noun or a verb; French seems to use negative structures more often than English does; German uses more subordination than Norwegian. In terms of textual strategies, we could rewrite these results in general terms like this:

> Change an abstract noun to a concrete noun.
> Change a noun to a verb.
> Change a negative to an affirmative.
> Change a subordination structure to a coordination structure.
> ...or vice versa, of course.

These then represent choices that a translator can make, depending of course on what languages are concerned, on the context, etc.

There are many textual strategies like this. And, as you would no doubt expect, they have been labelled and classified in many different ways.

EW

Hm, yes. Allow me to have a little rant about this foible. Why oh why can't language theorists, of all people, write in a standard language that everyone

can understand? Why do their pronouncements have to be "securely pro-
tected by the unbreakable code of academic language" as Malcolm Bradbury
has put (cit. Berglund 1990: 151)? Especially since we translators desperately need some kind of comprehensible metalanguage that we can use to
talk about our work and justify our strategies – to each other and to our clients? OK, not your fault. Let's hear more about textual strategies.

AC

Textual strategies

Here is one classification of textual strategies (Chesterman 1997: Ch. 4). A
strategy may be *obligatory*, required by contrastive differences between languages; or it may be *optional*.

SYNTACTIC STRATEGIES: purely syntactic changes of one kind or
another.

Literal translation
– Maximally close to the source-language form, but nevertheless grammatical.

Loan, calque
– The borrowing of individual items plus the borrowing of syntagma
(*Übermensch* $\Rightarrow$ *Superman*). Also includes 'double presentation': including both source-language and target-language terms in the translation, so
that one acts as a gloss of the other ($\Rightarrow$ *Duma, the Russian Parliament*).

Transposition
– Any change of word-class, e.g. from noun to verb, adjective to adverb.

Unit shift
– The units are: morpheme, word, phrase, clause, sentence, paragraph.
Obvious subclasses (e.g. a word translated as a phrase).

Phrase structure change
– Changes at the level of the phrase, including number, definiteness and
modification in the noun phrase, and person, tense and mood in the verb
phrase (e.g. a change from present to past tense).

Clause structure change
– Changes that have to do with the structure of the clause (e.g. change from
Subject-Verb-Object structure to Adverbial-Verb-Subject; changes between
active and passive, finite and non-finite, transitive and intransitive).

Sentence structure change
– Changes in the structure of the sentence-unit, insofar as it is made up of

---

clause-units; e.g. changes between main-clause and sub-clause status, changes of sub-clause types.

Cohesion change
– A change that affects intra-textual reference, ellipsis, substitution, pronominalization and repetition, or the use of connectors (e.g. adding or reducing cohesion markers).

Level shift
– Changes where the expression of a particular aspect of meaning moves from one level to another (the levels are phonology, morphology, syntax and lexis). These changes are usually obligatory ones (e.g. a change from a preposition to a case-ending).

Scheme change
– Changes that concern rhetorical schemes such as parallelism, repetition, alliteration, metrical rhythm, etc. Basic subtypes:
   (a) scheme X $\Rightarrow$ *scheme X* (e.g. repetition preserved from source to target text);
   (b) scheme X $\Rightarrow$ *scheme Y* (e.g. repetition changed to alliteration);
   (c) scheme X $\Rightarrow$ *scheme Ø* (e.g. repetition dropped, no replacing scheme);
   (d) scheme Ø $\Rightarrow$ *scheme X.*(e.g. repetition added, no scheme in the source text).

SEMANTIC STRATEGIES: changes concerning lexical, figurative and thematic meaning.

Synonymy
– The strategy of selecting not the 'obvious' equivalent but a synonym or near-synonym for it, e.g. to avoid repetition.

Antonymy
– Selecting an antonym plus a negation element (*good > pas mal*).

Hyponymy
– Changes within the hyponymy (inclusion) relation:
   (a) superordinate $\Rightarrow$ *hyponym (fleur* $\Rightarrow$ *tulip)*;
   (b) hyponym $\Rightarrow$ *superordinate (tulip* $\Rightarrow$ *fleur)*;
   (c) hyponym X $\Rightarrow$ *hyponym Y (of the same superordinate) (tulip* $\Rightarrow$ *jacinthe)*.

Converses
– Using the other member of a pair of (usually) verbal structures which

express the same state of affairs from opposing viewpoints, such as *buy* and *sell* (e.g. *He persuaded me* ⇒ *Je fus convaincu*).

Abstraction change
– Moving either from abstract to more concrete or from concrete to more abstract.

Distribution change
– Changes in the distribution of the 'same' semantic components over more items (expansion) or fewer items (compression) (e.g. *selon toute vraisemblance* ⇒ *probably*).

Emphasis change
– Changes in the emphasis or thematic focus.

Paraphrase
– Changes that result in a translation that can be described as loose, free, sometimes even 'undertranslated'.

Trope change
– Changes in the use of figurative expressions such as metaphors, personifications, etc. Subtypes:
    (a) trope X ⇒ *trope X* (e.g. personification preserved);
    (b) trope X ⇒ *trope Y* (e.g. personification replaced by a metaphor);
    (c) trope X ⇒ *trope Ø* (e.g. personification dropped, no replacing trope);
    (d) trope Ø ⇒ *trope* (e.g. personification added, no trope in the source text).

Other semantic changes
– Other changes of semantic nuance of various kinds.

PRAGMATIC STRATEGIES: concerning the selection of information in the target text.

Cultural filtering
– This strategy is also referred to as *naturalization, domestication* or *adaptation*. It describes the way in which source-language items, particularly culture-specific items, are translated as target-language cultural or functional equivalents, so that they conform to target-language norms. The opposite procedure, whereby such items are not adapted in this way but are, for example, borrowed or transferred directly, is thus *exoticization, foreignization* or *estrangement*.

Explicitness change
– Changes either towards more explicitness (*explicitation*) or towards more

implicitness (*implicitation*). Explicitation makes explicit certain information that is only implicit in the original. Implicitation omits information which the target readers can be reasonably expected to infer (see examples in Chapter 1 above).

Information change
– Either the addition of new (non-inferrable) information that is deemed to be relevant to the target readership but is not present in the source text, or the omission of source-text information deemed to be irrelevant (this latter might involve summarizing, for instance).

Interpersonal change
– Changes affecting the formality level, the degree of emotiveness and involvement, the level of technical lexis, etc. (e.g. the beginnings and ends of letters).

Illocutionary change
– Changes of speech act, e.g. involving a change of the mood of the verb from indicative to imperative, changes in the use of rhetorical questions and exclamations, changes between direct and indirect speech.

Coherence change
– Changes having to do with the logical arrangement of information in the text, e.g. in paragraphing.

Partial translation
– This covers any kind of partial translation, such as summary translation, transcription, translation of the sounds only.

Visibility change
– Changes in the status of the authorial presence, or concerning the overt intrusion or foregrounding of the translatorial presence; e.g. translator's footnotes, bracketed comments (such as explanations of puns) or added glosses.

Transediting
– Changes involving radical re-editing of the source text, e.g. because it is badly written.

Other pragmatic changes
– Changes such as layout or choice of dialect.

Research on these strategies deals with two general questions. The first is: what actually are the strategies? And the second is: under what conditions is each one used? The first question has been pretty well explored now. I think we have a reasonable overall picture of the various text-processing choices that a translator can make, despite disagreements about terminology. So we know what conceptual tools are available. But the second question is much harder to answer. We are only beginning to establish the conditions under which a particular strategy is used (or rather: used successfully). These conditions can be extremely complex, because so many variables are involved. Of course, we can make some guesses based on intuition or experience, or on an occasional case study, but we need more empirical evidence before we can make good predictions.

We know, for instance, that literal translation strategies are frequent in certain kinds of translations (e.g. legal texts), that adaptation strategies are frequent in other kinds of texts (e.g. children's literature). We also know quite a bit about strategies that seem to be compulsory (for translation between a given pair of languages) as compared with those that are optional (a matter of translator's choice and judgement). The compulsory ones are studied in contrastive linguistics, for instance, which is interested in the typical ways languages differ in expressing more or less the same meaning. Such differences have to do with the structure of the language, its rhetorical and stylistic conventions, and so on.

We can say, for instance, that structure X in language A very frequently gets translated into language B as structure Y – but this does not mean that every translator will always translate it that way, under all circumstances. (If we could make predictions that were always 100% accurate, we could program machines and retire to the Seychelles... Unfortunately, it's not that easy.)

Hence the difficulty of producing 'guidelines'. We can make general recommendations like 'think of the purpose' or 'be relevant', but these remain very abstract, as you have pointed out. We could also say: 'Hey, look at all these conceptual tools available; try some of these when you get stuck next time'. Would that count as a guideline? As a teacher, I hope that my students will at least become aware of the existence of a wide range of textual strategies during their studies. But professionals are probably familiar with them anyway, aren't they?

EW

Personally I think that if professionals get stuck, they will find the other strategies you mentioned – creativity strategies and search strategies – more useful than a list of textual strategies or conceptual tools. I'll explain later. What about the effects of textual strategies?

AC

To recommend a strategy is to predict an effect: if you translate this bit (this kind of thing) like this (using this strategy), I predict that the client will like it / the reader will understand better / the translation will have the desired effect. But predicting effects is notoriously difficult in the human sciences. OK, I can predict some obvious ones – so can anyone, with a bit of common sense. If you use this loanword, many readers will be puzzled. If you write ungrammatically, clients will throw your text out (if they read it). If you omit that negation, people will do the wrong thing when they tune their new television. But in order to be able to predict that readers will find structure A easier to understand than structure B, or that textual strategy X will have a better effect than strategy Y, I need evidence from reader response studies, psycholinguistics, behavioural research, and so on.

Digressive example of a prediction: Here is an extract from the monthly journal *Prospect* (May 1999), their 'Brussels Diary' column.

> [German foreign minister] Joschka Fischer was presenting a draft statement on Nato's intervention in Serbia for all 15 EU nations to sign, insisting that Nato's military action against Serbia is *both necessary and justified*. The EU's four non-Nato members – Sweden, Finland, Austria and Ireland – all squirmed. Finland's [foreign minister] Tarja Halonen said that in her language, the word for *justified* had strong judicial implications, and she could not endorse it. "How about *warranted*?" suggested [British foreign minister] Robin Cook, and Joschka Fischer nodded; that was fine with him. Belgium's Erik Derycke and France's Hubert Védrine raised amused eyebrows, knowing that the French text would still carry the word *justifié*.

'Strong judicial implications' – in other words, the effect would be a political storm in Finland. Unless, of course, the Finnish translator used a different term: not the obvious Finnish equivalent for *justified* (in Finnish: *oikeutettu*, a derivation from *oikeus*, 'justice') but a more general term meaning 'motivated, having a good reason' (Finnish: *perusteltu*, from *perus* 'basis'). This strategy could be labelled synonymy: use a near-synonym, not the closest possible equivalent to the original. An alternative classification might call this an example of one kind of *hyponymy* strategy: use a more general term (a hyperonym) instead of a more specific one (a hyponym).

EW

Surely, the problem is one of undesirable connotations. Ms Halonen wanted to avoid the word *justified* because she knew it would be translated as *oikeutettu* in Finnish – by translators producing the Finnish version of the statement, and also subconsciously by educated Finnish readers reading the official statement in English or French. There are at least two things wrong with *oikeutettu* in this context. As you say, it is derived from *oikeus*, 'justice'; also it is exactly the same word as in the Finnish expression for 'a just war' (*oikeutettu sota*) and therefore possibly undesirable in this context. Because

English has two slightly different words ('justified' and 'just war'), as does French ('justifié' and 'guerre juste'), the connotations are not quite as strong in those languages.

AC

So far, explicit research into translation effects has rather tended to focus on the wider effects, at the cultural and social levels, of different kinds of translation strategies. These include effects such as how the receiving culture then perceives the source culture, and vice versa. Postcolonial and feminist scholars have a lot to say here (see, for example, Robinson 1997b).

But surely effects at this cultural level are of concern to you too, as you labour away at your wordface? Readers who get a text they can understand without too much effort will think differently about the source culture and the sender of the text, compared with readers who are presented with gobbledegook.

What you would like to see, I guess, is a series of studies along the lines of problem-solving guidelines: for problem type X, here are the basic strategies that have 'good' effects, and here are the main conditions of use for each one. I agree – this kind of research would be most valuable. Perhaps the most studied problem type to date in this respect is the translation of metaphors (see Newmark 1988: ch.10; Toury 1995: 81f) – but this might not be at the top of your list of priorities?

Standard solutions for translating metaphors
(classification and examples adapted from Newmark 1988):

* Reproducing the same metaphor, the same image
    (ray of hope ⇒ rayon d'espoir)
* Using a different metaphor, a different image
    (other fish to fry ⇒ d'autres chats à fouetter)
* Using a simile (i.e. a different rhetorical device)
    (La fenice è Dorabella ⇒ Dorabella is like the Phoenix of Arabia)
* Using a simile plus a paraphrase to give the sense
    (C'est un renard ⇒ He is as sharp and cunning as a fox)
* Using a paraphrase alone, with no rhetorical device
    (gagner son pain ⇒ earn one's living)
* Deletion: omit the whole bit.
* Literal translation plus a gloss
    (A Biblical example, from James ch. 3, verse 6: "The tongue is a fire".
    A translator might then add an explanatory gloss to show the sense:
    "Our words can destroy things, like a fire destroys things".)

Choosing the appropriate solution depends on many factors: the kind of metaphor (original, cliché...), text type, global translation strategy, and the time available.

EW

Anything practical, concrete and non-coercive would be welcome. Translators need to be able to choose between several alternatives. So I am beginning to understand why a narrowly prescriptive approach would be undesirable: there are too many variables to be able to impose any particular textual strategy.

We have, then, agreed that it is impossible to prescribe translation solutions, and therefore to program machines and retire to the Seychelles. So what makes you think you can 'predict translation effects'? This idea seems impossibly ambitious – a drain on research funds almost as bottomless as the pit into which cash has been poured in pursuit of reliable machine translation. Before you can predict the 'wider effects' of translations, you surely need to be able to measure and predict the effect of writing as such – and who can do that? In my experience it has less to do with the words you write than with the preconceptions of readers and their perception of the author. Readers' perceptions of what I write in this book, for example, will be influenced by the fact that I am a translator, that my mother tongue is English, that I am female, a Eurocrat... plenty of room for prejudice and preconceptions there!

AC

I agree that predicting effects can only be done rather vaguely and generally, and that translation effects overlap with the effects of any kind of writing. If I use non-standard English in a translation of an academic article, for instance, I can reasonably predict that many readers will not like this, they will react negatively.

Perhaps we should talk rather of applying what we can find out from empirical studies. Suppose, for instance, that we study the reactions of clients and readers to the use of certain kinds of translation strategies under certain conditions. How tolerant are clients/readers of the use of loanwords, or translator's notes, or translator's stylistic improvements, or the translator's choice of a general domesticating or foreignizing approach? Information on such matters might then help us to predict whether the use of a given strategy in a particular case might be acceptable or not.

EW

Can we come back to the other problem-solving strategies you mentioned – creativity strategies and search strategies? Some colleagues of mine (Bill Fraser and Helen Titchen 1998) have produced a list of what they call *distancing strategies* based on input from professional translators. This suggests that the best way of getting unstuck is to put some distance between yourself and the actual words you are trying to translate, as follows:

****

DISTANCING

This section describes some of the strategies for distancing that are actually used by professional translators. Because these strategies are drawn from day-to-day practice, most translators are likely to be using something similar already. The crucial part is becoming consciously aware of WHAT you are doing and HOW, and deliberately applying that awareness in order to develop even more effective working routines.

1. What do we mean by distancing?
Distancing is something all translators, and indeed most other creative people, know about. It means stepping back mentally from what you are creating to get a better perspective on it.
  We do this for all sorts of reasons, which include:
* understanding what the source text is saying;
* getting inspiration for formulating the target text;
* carrying out research;
* improving on our first version;
* final checking of our final handiwork.

One essential characteristic of distancing appears to be a deliberate kind of artificial 'forgetting', a 'clearing of the mental screen' – forgetting what you were thinking when you created the target text, even forgetting it was you who created it, forgetting what you know already in order to get a 'naive' and fresh view of difficulties, and so on.
Clearly, being more aware of distancing techniques and knowing how to use them more consciously is a valuable resource for any self-respecting translator.

2. Distancing when producing the translation
Translators report the following strategies for gaining distance from both the source text and their draft translation during the translating process. The general idea is that short-term memory becomes overlaid with other impressions and you can return to the translation with new eyes.

* Plan to insert small breaks at frequent intervals
Examples:
(When dictating) put down the microphone, play back your dictation and just listen.
(When working on screen) save document and check back for errors, do necessary research on the source text, consult a colleague about a problem in the text, make phone calls, etc.

* Make a longer break by sharing the job with other people
Examples:
(Dictating) while the audiotypist is typing your dictation, you can do your research, work on a different translation, write up terminology, etc.
(Screen working) turn over the translation to an audiotypist to put in your hand-written corrections, etc.

*Stop work on the current job and do a different type of task for a while
   Examples:
   Do a different translation
   Revise a translation
   Make terminology notes
   Add new material to your computer aids
   Read your e-mail
   Do some administrative form filling!

* Leave the translation overnight to look at in the morning
Like the last point, this is a matter of personal organization of work and its different phases. You can arrange the translating task so that the night away from the text comes at the point where it is most effective.

* Practise changing your internal state when you want
The ability to change your state at will is a very useful skill to have on those occasions when you cannot afford the time to make a complete break and stop the translation altogether.
   Examples:
   Come out of your creative thinking state and
   (screen working) check systematically for surface detail such as spelling and syntax errors, or
   (dictating) critically consider style, clarity and so on of the translation
   so far;
   Listen to or read back over your translation as if you were the target
   audience, or as if this were someone else's work you are revising.
Here a little play-acting is very useful: you can change internal state by sitting in a different chair or going to another room (e.g. have a 'creative' chair for translating and a 'critic's' chair for reading it through).

3. Distancing by consulting another person
The trick here is to use the distance from the text which an outside person has but which you have lost by becoming too 'intimate' with it. For instance, because you must translate with constant reference to the source text, you might not notice that your translation does not stand up on its own (as it must do when it reaches the target audience) but only makes sense when read side-by-side with the source text.

* A fellow-translator of your language
Give your problem source passage to a fellow-translator of your language to read. Do this without explaining where you perceive a difficulty. They will either confirm that they see the same problem and help you towards a solu-tion, or they may see no problem and give you the solution. Alternatively, of course, they may see an entirely different problem which you had not even noticed!
   The whole point is not to spoil the 'freshness' of your colleague's distance by explaining too much beforehand.

Alternatively, read your translation of the passage out loud to a fellow-translator. When you do this, indicate the general context without letting them read either the source text or your translation. Your colleague functions like the target audience of the document, as a check that a well-formed meaning is being conveyed. Only then show them the source text as a cross-check.

The reason for reading the translation out loud rather than showing the passage is to further preserve the other person's ignorance and therefore distance from the problem.

* A fellow-translator of the language of the source text
Show your problem passage to a fellow-translator of the language of the source text. Ask them for a paraphrase of the meaning. Having two versions in the original language to compare may help you to see an aspect of meaning that you had not considered before; if they have trouble paraphrasing, this confirms that the source text is not clear (and that the author should be contacted).

* The author or a terminologist
Contact the author or a terminologist. Identify the problem passage, then paraphrase your understanding of the source passage and ask them for feedback.

The author can confirm if that is the intended meaning or not.

The terminologist may also be able to confirm your understanding, but is more likely to question you further about the context and where your real problem lies, clarifying the contextual meaning for you and helping you towards a solution.

* Your friendly office ghost...
Simply imagine explaining your problem with the text to someone else (translator, author). This is not as wacky as it sounds: being clear in your own mind about what the problem is may well produce a step towards part or all of the solution.

4. Distancing in problem-solving
Distancing in problem-solving usually means seeing the problem in a new light (a new context). There are two broad categories of problem: comprehension of the source text and formulation in the target text.

* Put yourself in the place of the author
What are you, the author, trying to say? What needs of the reader are you trying to satisfy? Understanding the author's purpose can unlock the probably intended meaning.

* Read another document on the same subject
The effect is similar to generating a paraphrase to compare and contrast with your source text. You may need to read something in the source or the target language depending on what kind of problem – comprehension or formulation – you have.

* Change your surroundings

You may not always have time to go to the cafeteria or walk the corridors, but you could pace about your office, sit on your windowsill or go to the library for inspiration.

* Change the medium

Try writing possible solutions down on a piece of paper and playing with them. If you're dictating, try writing or typing, if you're working on screen, try reading or speaking out loud.

* Get your subconscious working

When struggling with the source text (problems of comprehension), you may understand just enough to continue translating; most translators find that their subconscious mind then carries on working on the unresolved questions and that solutions can spring into consciousness unexpectedly later.

Try to cultivate this by identifying the types of problem that can safely be 'sent downstairs' and trusting the 'unseen workshop' of your brain.

* Change state from 'cogitate' to 'contemplate'

When searching for inspiration (problems of formulation), remember that inspiration resides in the unconscious mind: try adopting a still, contemplative state:

> sit back in your chair,
>
> rid yourself of excess muscle tension,
>
> deepen your breathing,
>
> de-focus your eyes,
>
> turn down your internal dialogue...

and allow the answer to emerge rather than consciously building it up brick by brick.

5. Distancing when reading through and polishing

This is the point in the translating process when distancing really comes into its own.

* Learning to forget

Discover consciously for yourself what is different in your experience when you read through your own translation and when you read something (which you did not write yourself) for the first time.

Specifically, notice changes in your body posture, physiology, and internal reading strategies (for example, do you pronounce the words silently in your mind in one context and not in the other? Are you seeing what is actually there, or are you seeing what you think SHOULD be there).

Once you have discovered what makes the difference, apply the 'first-time' strategy when reading through your translations.

* Change the medium

Dictating: After hearing yourself dictate the text onto tape, what a revelation to read it on paper. All the awkward passages seem to stand out! The tape has also been with the audiotypist for a while, so you have forgotten the detail of your thought processes.

Screen-working: Although you could teach yourself to do your final checking on screen, you may prefer to correct a print-out on paper. You can also read the translation out loud to yourself or someone else or get them to read it back to you.

* Start reading at some point in the middle of the document
Many of the cues that trigger memories of what you were thinking when translating can be bypassed by breaking up the logic of the text and its sequential argument.

* Give the translation to someone else to read or imagine you are that other person
It is not usually considered acceptable to leave *all* your final checking and correcting to a reviser, but you could agree beforehand with a colleague to work in just that way, or at least read out short passages to another translator to get their reaction.

Alternatively, you can imagine you are the reviser or intended reader of the document, perhaps reading aloud to yourself (in a foreign accent?).

* Adopt a regular final checking routine
You can invent a whole ritual for final checking that distinguishes it from translating (start by sitting in another chair, etc.).

Objects can be invested with 'switching power', e.g. some revisers switch on their more critical 'revision frame of mind' just by picking up a red pen!

* Separate the tasks involved
There are at least four features to check for:

> completeness,
> accuracy of spelling, numbers and formatting,
> clarity of syntax and style,
> transmission of the message.

Each of these can be made into a separate pass through the text to avoid working on several mental levels at once and so missing some errors.

****

AC

That's an interesting list. Sounds like your colleagues are well into lateral thinking: I guess De Bono (1977) would say your 'distancing' means different ways of thinking laterally, looking at something from a different perspective. The idea about changing one's internal state (your optimism is most moving!) also makes me think of neurolinguistic programming (NLP).

Many of the suggestions you list will ring a bell with translators, I agree. They seem to cover both what I called search strategies and creative strategies.

I suspect that future research on professional translators' time management and different working processes will shed further light on the kinds of things translators do in order to achieve a distancing effect. It is a pity that not much research along these lines has been published, as far as I know. This is one of the directions that future empirical research may well take. (You might, of course, retort that, from your point of view, this is where we should have started, rather than with abstractions, etc.)

The point about reading another document is an important one. Since the 1970s or so, with the increasing influence of text linguistics, translation scholars have talked about two kinds of relevant 'other documents' (see Neubert and Shreve 1992). One kind is what we call *parallel texts*. (Actually, I mentioned these briefly in Chapter 3.) These are target-language texts that are on the same subject matter as a particular source text, not translations but naturally occurring texts in the target culture. They ideally have the same kind of style and function, too. So if you are translating a patent, for instance, you might want to look at non-translated target-language patents in the same field, to get an idea of the kind of vocabulary and stylistic features that tend to be used.

The second kind of other document is what some scholars call *background texts*. These form a wider and more heterogeneous group than parallel texts. Background texts include anything at all that is written in the target language on roughly the same subject: they could be newspaper articles, encyclopedia entries, websites, introductions to the subject 'for the intelligent layman', university textbooks, etc.

It seems that as translators become more experienced, they tend to rely less on dictionaries and more on parallel and background texts in their search for the *mot juste*.

EW

Dictionaries, yes. Or rather, no. I think this is the first time we've mentioned them in this book. Which might seem strange to non-initiates who think translation is all about looking things up in a dictionary.

As you say, real documents are of more use to translators than dictionaries. Least-loved is the *multilingual dictionary* without contexts or definitions, with entries like this:

>   EN: *window*
>   FR: *fenêtre* (f)
>   DE: *Fenster* (n)
>   IT: *finestra* (f)
>   etc.

General *bilingual dictionaries* have their place in language learning, but when you've attained reasonable proficiency in a foreign language you won't need them very often (and if you haven't attained that level of proficiency, you shouldn't be translating it professionally). We all like to have a good bilingual dictionary as back-up, of course. Next come the *specialized bilingual dictionaries.* Some are worthless, because they get out-of-date very quickly, and usually don't give definitions, but there are some excellent ones on technical and financial subjects (as a general rule, the narrower the field they cover, the more reliable they are likely to be). Most useful of all are *monolingual dictionaries* (one good general dictionary for the source language, another for the target). Translators use these more than multilingual or bilingual dictionaries, for example when we come across an unfamiliar word or need a precise definition. Of course most dictionaries are now in CD-ROM or other electronic formats – quicker and easier to search.

On-line terminology collections are often more useful than dictionaries because new material can be added all the time, and they can be searched easily even when they are very large. Actually, electronic text searching has made dictionary-style alphabetic word lists superfluous. Which brings us to full-text searching and our preference for real documents. Large electronic archives and the Internet have transformed translators' lives by opening up access to huge volumes of parallel and background texts. I will say more about this in Chapter 7.

On the subject of professional translators' working methods, could you tell me if theoretical research using think-aloud protocols has produced any useful findings? I understand that the idea is to get translators to talk through the translation and thus explain the process. Surely it is difficult to verbalize one's thought processes when the translation is still at a non-verbal or pre-verbal stage?

AC

Think-aloud protocols (TAPs) began to be used in translation research in the 1980s (useful survey articles are Kussmaul and Tirkkonen-Condit 1995; Jääskeläinen 1998). Yes, the idea is that you ask translators to speak aloud while they translate, and record what they say. You can also coordinate this recorded protocol with a computer time-record of keystrokes, so you can see exactly where they pause, for how long, where they delete, etc. Or you record the whole process on videotape.

The method has obvious weaknesses, which have been much discussed: e.g. that translators will behave in an untypical way if they have to talk aloud and if they are being watched; that they cannot talk about everything that comes into their minds anyway but must select; that they cannot talk about what they are not aware of; that they will just say what they think the observer wants to hear; and so on.

Researchers have tried to be aware of these problems, and to cope with them as best they can. For instance, subjects practise the TAP process thoroughly before they are recorded, which helps them talk more naturally. And results are often better if the subjects work in pairs, talking more naturally to each other. (But, say the critics, translators rarely actually work in pairs, so this is unnatural too.) Protocol data can also be supplemented with follow-up interview data.

You ask about the results of this kind of research. Well, it's early days yet. Transcribing the data is very laborious, and numbers of subjects in a given experiment have been very few. Much of the work has compared trainee translators with more experienced ones, trying to pinpoint things that might be useful for translator training. Here are a few examples of what has come up so far.

* Processing a text does not proceed in a linear way. Translators return to earlier solutions, change them, then return to where they were, then go back again, and so on. There are lots of recursive movements.
* Processing is not smooth. There seems to be a clear difference between bits of the translation that come easily, automatically, and bits that translators have to pause and think about. These are the bits they usually talk about, of course. Studies that follow the translator's eye-movements confirm this jerkiness.
* There also seems to be a difference between the way translators deal with texts that are routine for them, and texts that are more unusual.
* Professionals use bilingual dictionaries much less than non-professionals.
* Professionals tend to mention the readers and the function of the translation more often than trainees do, they are more oriented towards the text as a whole; trainees tend more to talk about the meanings of source-text items, details.
* Professionals in general raise more problems, they are more aware of possible difficulties.
* There seems to be some correlation between the emotional state of the translator and the resulting quality of the translation: bad moods, irritation or depression do not make for high quality.
* The self-image of the translator, and their attitude towards the job, also seem to have an effect on quality. Translators who repeatedly moan about their own weaknesses or lack of knowledge tend to produce translations that are less good than translators who are more confident of their skills.
* A high level of personal involvement in the subject-matter of the text also seems to go with higher quality. Translators who are less interested in a particular text tend to do less well.

Results such as these are no more than suggestive, of course. I think the apparent importance of emotive and attitudinal factors is interesting, though.

EW

The protocol research results seem to reflect what would be termed 'common knowledge' by most translators. No doubt scholars would be loath to use common knowledge as a basis for their theorizing, and prefer to have it confirmed by research. But I was surprised when you said these studies were carried out 'to pinpoint things that might be useful for translator training'. Not so pure and abstract after all, then? If research is taking this practical turn, how about further think-aloud protocol studies to compare:
* productive and unproductive professional translators?;
* different professional translators' research strategies, faced by the same text?

AC

The second has already been taken up by scholars working with this methodology, but I am not aware of work comparing productive and unproductive professionals. Do you have any unproductive colleagues who might be willing to act as informants?

EW

I'm sure a full range of informants can be found. I wonder if the results would reveal anything new, or just confirm common knowledge?

AC

On common knowledge as a basis for theorizing: I suspect that academics respect this kind of knowledge more than you might think, but as a source of hypotheses rather than a fount of truth. Unless what they are interested in is precisely 'common knowledge per se', i.e. *folk knowledge*. There is, for instance, research on the man-in-the-street's concept of translation itself: this turns out to be a typical fuzzy, prototype concept, with more typical and less typical characteristics, rather than a clear and well-defined concept.

EW

Surely there is a difference between 'common knowledge' of the type shared by expert insiders, and 'folk knowledge' or the misinformed preconceptions of the man-in-the-street? As long as you have a good self-image, who cares about the folk image? Take the typical folk image of academic writing, which would probably be something like this: 'After you've filtered out all the jargon, and condensed all the clouds of hot air, you end up with a small drop of information so banal that you wonder why you (and the author) bothered'.

Most translators-in-the-street are terrible cynics, and they often express similarly scathing views of the material they translate. Recently one of my Dutch colleagues complained that he'd just translated a 60-page report whose message could be distilled into three sentences: 'Poverty is a bad thing. It is getting worse. We must do something about it'.

Whether or not such cynicism is healthy, the translator's mood and attitude are important, as the protocol research results showed. Everyone has their off days, in any job, and translators are no exception. If you spend most of your working life – day in, day out – engaged in a demanding mental activity like translation, you have to decide where to cut corners, and where an extra intellectual effort is worthwhile. Many choices have to be made, not just 'Which is the best turn of phrase?', but 'Where can I find out more about this subject? In the archives? On the Internet? By asking a colleague? By asking an expert? Which is the quickest route to the right answer? Will I miss the deadline if I keep on searching? Is it worth even trying? Does it matter? Can I fudge it somehow? Who will notice? Will they care?', etc.

Maybe what professional translators need, in addition to textual strategies, creative strategies and research strategies, are *motivation* strategies.

AC

Agreed. This means we need to look at translating not so much as a purely linguistic activity but in a socio-psychological framework, governed by emotions and power relations, etc. From this point of view, self-image and self-confidence are central concepts. One theoretical idea that might be helpful here is that of the *habitus*, developed by the French sociologist Pierre Bourdieu (see Simeoni 1998; Hermans 1999).

Bourdieu defines a **habitus** as a set of dispositions that characterize an agent acting in a field. Sorry – I'll unpack that backwards. A field is this sense is a sociological area, a structured space in which a given social activity takes place. There is thus a field we can call 'translation' in which various people are involved in the activity of translating. Any field is criss-crossed by power relations, and functions according to given laws or norms or conventions. An agent is anyone acting in a field. Agents in the translation field include translators, clients, heads of translation agencies, secretaries, revisers, text producers, etc. A disposition is a tendency to think, feel or act in a particular way. Collect a group of dispositions that are shared by a group of agents, and you have a habitus. So a translator's habitus is something like the general emotional and cognitive state of mind and self-image of a typical translator, together with typical associated behaviour patterns, as shaped by the tradition of power relations in the field of translation. (Are you still with me?)

Now comes the interesting bit. It seems that the typical translator's habitus is actually rather depressing. Daniel Simeoni describes it as a habitus of "voluntary servitude" (1998: 23). Theo Hermans asks: "Are translators born subservient, do they acquire subservience, or do they have subservience thrust upon them?" (1999: 134). Translators serve their clients, of course, and it is the clients who usually have the most power. But translators also seem prone to reinforce their submissive status by their own habitual practice. They are not as aware as they might be of their own power to influence these practices, little by little. If you only follow the norms, you strengthen them even further. But if you resist them, and experiment with alternatives (say the scholars), and if your experiments are taken up by other translators, and then still others – then you can be influential in setting up new norms. Your Fight the Fog campaign seems a good example of this. It might even change the EU translator's habitus.

So one advantage of the habitus idea is that it can help to highlight the affective aspect of the translator's work, the importance of self-image. Another is the way it makes us aware of the power relations that it is governed by, and hence raises the possibility of questioning these power relations. This in turn might have some effect on motivation.

Talking of which, surely one of the best motivation strategies is the use of professional quality time. By this, I mean time away from routine work but nevertheless given to professional issues. In Bourdieu's terms, this means a shift of agent role but within the same field. For example, suppose a professional translator is given a month off to work as an exchange teacher in a university, in one of the countries where one of his professional languages is spoken. As you know, we have some good experience of this in Finland, with visiting EU translators coming to teach and participate in seminars, etc., as well as brush up their Finnish. Such possibilities should be more widely available.

Alternatively, a translator might shift to the role of a reviser, or an organizer, for a month or so, to taste a different power, or even start writing a book... After all, translators do not absolutely have to see themselves as being in voluntary servitude permanently.

EW

So it looks as if we need two kinds of motivation strategies:

* *local* ('How do I get through this document without losing the will to live?' Usual answer: 'Think about pay day'. Organizing a clear writing campaign takes a little longer.);
* *global*, of the kind you mention.

No doubt you realize that the motivation strategies you advocate are all forms of *distancing* (see the section above). Changing over temporarily to revision, teaching, management – these are all ways of stepping back so you can see things in proportion and return refreshed. They are all useful; but it would be a shame (and a waste of valuable resources) if we always had to stop translating in order to motivate ourselves to carry on. And in a way it just confirms the 'menial routine subservience' image, rather than changing it. Recently, when asked what would motivate them, many of my colleagues said 'more time' and 'longer deadlines' (the same thing) or 'appreciation' and 'feedback' (also the same thing – critical feedback not required, thanks). One of the most interesting replies came from a Spanish translator and philosophy graduate, who said that she was already motivated: by 'the feeling that I am respected by my colleagues and readers'. And when asked how she avoided boredom, she mentioned another distancing technique – variety. Translating a different sort of text, using a different translation method for a change, maybe even a different translation tool (more on this in Chapter 7).

Respect and variety – I'm not sure what, if anything, they have to do with power relations. Bourdieu seems, like some of the other scholars you've mentioned, to be excessively interested in asserting individuality. Surely he has read his compatriot J.-J. Rousseau's *Du Contrat social* and is familiar with the idea of surrendering one's individual power in the interests of collective – and greater – achievement. To show what I mean, why not look at some other agents and the fields they act in? Take musicians: what is one to make of their habitus? A tone-deaf observer would probably find musicians dreadfully subservient. Not only do they slavishly follow a score written hundreds of years ago, but they have to do it in time with all the other musicians in the orchestra, and they might not even get their name on the record case. With all due respect to Bourdieu, who cares about power? Listen to the music!

6. Is it any good?

AC

You said, at the end of Chapter 5, 'Who cares about power?'. Well, many translation scholars do, nowadays. They are interested in the ways translators and translations manipulate power, and also how they are influenced by power relations. For many of us, this aspect of translation raises interesting and problematic ethical issues concerning responsibility, ideology, values.

We thought we would call this chapter 'Is it any good?', but maybe that is too narrow. What about the question of 'good' translation in a wider sense? How should I behave ethically as a translator? What is ethically good practice? What ethical justification can I appeal to, as I try to understand my own behaviour and decisions as a translator? I think these questions will bring us back again to the big issues we looked at earlier, concerning the need felt by translators to justify their very existence as translators, at least in their own minds, to themselves.

But let's start with the more usual sense of 'good translation'. What kinds of criteria do you work with? Is it enough simply to accept that the client always right?

EW

Let's leave the big issues of ethics and power until later. There are enough basic problems with translation quality. Perhaps starting with the point, which we made in Chapter 3, that good translation is invisible. You only notice a translation if there's something wrong with it. And then perhaps moving on to the next problem: there is never any one correct translation. The original text is final, fixed and immutable; but the translation is a fluid, perfectible thing. Translations can vary over time (successive translations of the Bible), depending on the purpose, the audience, the translator's skill – even the same translator may translate a text differently at different times, depending on inspiration, fatigue, stress...

Yet quality assessment is central to translation. It is what we do to ourselves all the time (Will this do? Does it mean the same as the original? Can I find a better way of expressing it?). It is what we do to other translators, checking, criticizing and pillaging their work. It is what others do to us: teachers, during our training, potential employers, deciding whether to recruit us; revisers, deleting our best efforts; and, finally, readers and end users of our translations.

In our 'industrial' context we encounter all sorts of views on translation quality and how to measure it:

1. Translation is a *product*. Just grade the end product: good, bad or indifferent.
2. Translation is a *process*. Quality depends on carrying out the process correctly.

3. Translation is a *service*, intangible but wholly dependent on customer satisfaction. Just measure customer satisfaction.
4. Translations are an *adjunct of the original text* – a more or less flawed image, "like a reproduction of a Rembrandt original in black and white" as Johan Huizinga said (cit. *Language Today* 1998: 21). Just measure the accuracy, the faithfulness to the original, the equivalence of meaning and effect.

The trouble is that 1, 2, 3 and 4 are all right. Translation *is* a product, a process and a service, and also a copy that cannot be judged without looking at the original. That's why quality assessment is so complicated – especially if it is to be objective and reproducible.

So to come back to your question 'Is it enough simply to accept that the client is always right?', the simple answer is 'No'. The client's opinion matters, of course, but as I said in Chapter 4, client is a blanket term for:

* the author, who may or may not understand the translation;
* the reader, who usually doesn't understand the original;
* a middleman between the two, usually preoccupied by deadlines and layout.

Authors often have very strange views on translation quality. I remember our wasted efforts to translate the slogan *Ensemble contre le dopage dans le sport*. The translator racked his brains for a snappy English equivalent. Then he saw the illustration that went with the slogan: it showed a footballer kicking a ball. So, in a flash of inspiration, he came up with *Let's kick doping out of sport*. But the author was unimpressed, opining that *ensemble* ('together') – an important word in the EU context – was not correctly conveyed. And he had the last word, so the English slogan became *Let's work together to kick doping out of sport*.

Readers are not entirely reliable judges of translation quality, but they can certainly assess the translation as a piece of writing. Usually they compare it with parallel texts that are not translations ('What this Japanese news item would say if it had been written in English, in a British newspaper...'). Occasionally they go too far, and reject perfectly accurate translations as 'pretentious translationese'. I shall never forget the secretary who re-typed a translation about dust control in coalmines, changing 'wetting agent' to 'water' throughout.

Are there any fair and objective ways of measuring readers' satisfaction with translation quality?

AC

I like your point that quality assessment is something we do to ourselves as we translate. It reminds me of Anthony Pym's definition of translation competence (in Pym 1992b: 175ff.), which goes roughly like this: a translator needs two abilities (apart from obvious language skills, etc.). One is the ability to come up with several possibilities, several potential equivalents. The second is the ability to select the best one, for the purpose in hand. The first skill needs divergent intelligence, imagination, creativity; the second needs convergent intelligence, the ability to criticize, analyze, compare, assess. When we do our own quality assessment – either in the head, as we think of various versions before writing anything, or on screen or paper as we revise – we are using precisely this second ability.

EW

Which in turn reminds me of what some of my colleagues have called 'the Disney creativity strategy'. Perhaps I should have mentioned it in Chapter 5 – but it is relevant here too.

One of Walt Disney's animators said of him: "There were actually three different Walts – the dreamer, the realist and the spoiler. You never knew which one was coming into your meeting" (in Thomas and Johnson 1981: 379). This neatly sums up the idea that there are not just two types of skill, but three skills or 'modes' in any creative process:

1. The 'dreamer' mode, in which creative options are generated;
2. The 'realist' mode, in which feasible options are selected and executed;
3. The 'critic' mode, whose function is to refine and improve the results of the previous two phases.

Each of these modes is of great value to the end result, but it is important that they should be kept separate (or taught to interact civilly!) and not be allowed to impinge upon each other. The dreamer, in particular, cannot function with the critic constantly interrupting.

In translation, the dreamer generates the initial conceptual formulation. The realist carries out the task of creating the translation in physical form. That's the persona that knows how to use a dictaphone or word processor. The realist also makes the translation viable, getting you from one end of the text to the other without skipping paragraphs. The spoiler (also called the 'inner critic') is the one who really turns the first draft into a valuable translation (with occasional help from the dreamer and the realist, to invent and test better alternatives).

AC

The more successful we are at doing this 'internal' or pre-deadline quality assessment, the less reason there will be for the client or original author or someone else to intervene – well, in principle, at least. Opinions can always differ...

In the tradition of translation studies, measuring the reactions of readers (in the sense of 'people who read the translation because they probably cannot read the original') has only been one way of trying to get at the more general question of 'how can we measure translation quality'. At least three other general approaches have been proposed. These all depend in some sense on readers' reactions, of course – but here the readers are not general ones, but a particular subset of them: scholars, critics and teachers. These are people whose special interest it is to evaluate translations. They are therefore not typical readers, not 'naive' readers. And this can sometimes give rise to problems: the judgements of this special group may not always be representative of the opinions of the wider readership for whom a translation is intended.

Here are the four basic approaches that we find in translation theory (they are discussed in more detail in my book, Chesterman 1997: Ch. 5); there are some obvious links with the views of translation quality that you mention above:

1. Comparing the translation with the source text. This approach sees the translation as a product (like your views 1 and 4). It has been much used by scholars and teachers for hundreds of years. There are many suggestions for analytical schemas, ways of classifying errors of equivalence, measuring loss of meaning, changes of meaning or style, etc. And there are also suggestions about how to assess the relative gravity of such errors, which have long been used in teaching and in testing.

2. Comparing the translation with parallel texts (that is, texts of a similar type in the target language, which are original, not translated). You mention that the general reader often reacts in this way. It is often easy to notice that a text 'reads like a translation' because it does not sound quite natural in some way. Modern research using computer corpora has tried to specify some of the evidence that underlies these readers' intuitions. Some interesting hypotheses have been discussed, dealing with quantitative differences between translations and originals in the same language. We are beginning to have some ideas about possible universal features of translations, regardless of the language (see Laviosa-Braithwaite 1998). Scholars find this interesting, because it might reveal something about the cognitive processes involved in processing texts from one language to another, and that in turn might suggest something about how the human brain works. However, we should remember that not all translations necessarily aim to sound totally natural in the target language; there may be more important priorities.

3. Measuring the reactions of general, typical readers. There has been some experimental work measuring things like:
   * time taken to read a translation (as compared with a matched original text);
   * ease of understanding (e.g. using comprehension tests or fill-in-the-missing-words tests);
   * performance (time and efficiency in following instructions, translations compared to matched original texts); and even

    * mental associations (to see how the connotations of a word might dif-
      fer from the connotations of an equivalent in another language).
In this approach, a translation is seen as part of a causal process: it causes
reactions in the reader's mind or behaviour.

4. Trying to get at the decision-making process during the translating itself.
Some people think that you can only judge the quality of a translation fairly if
you know why the translator translated that way, why they made a particular
decision. In order to find out this you need to ask the translator, or to do a
protocol analysis (see Chapter 5).

    The view you mentioned of translation being a service, so quality assess-
ment must depend on customer satisfaction, has had less attention in academic
translation studies, but certainly underlies proposals coming from the translation industry, about translation quality standards.

EW

In fact most industrial quality standards are process-related, with client feedback playing only a small part in the process. They aim to ensure customer
satisfaction by laying down the rules for getting the process right (or, at the
very least, getting the most important part of the process right: choosing a
qualified translator). Active research into customer satisfaction only makes
sense when you have a reasonably stable customer base, a uniform source
of supply and a fairly large translation turnover. This is the case in large organizations such as the EU institutions. And yes, we do occasionally hold
'user-satisfaction surveys', formal or informal, to see how our in-house clients rate the service they are receiving. Their comments reveal a striking and
depressing fact: they take linguistic quality for granted. What they are really
interested in is deadlines. When we receive praise, it is because we have
performed an impossible feat – translating fifty pages in three hours, for instance. And as our customers constantly remind us, an imperfect translation
delivered on time is far better that a perfect one delivered late.
    Other elements contributing to the quality of the 'service package' here
are: correct layout and computer format, advice on corrections needed in the
original (if it contains mistakes) and multilingual concordance (to ensure that
all the translations match).
    Standards for the translation industry are of several types, all beneficial
because they attempt to regulate what is still an unregulated profession, and
to introduce some quality safeguards for both clients and translators. But
none of the existing standards lays down any criteria for measuring translation quality. Some standards, like ISO-9002 and DIN 2345, are mainly
process-related. They are based on the assumption that if the correct procedures are followed, reliable translations will result. Others are more like
accreditation schemes (such as UNI 10574 in Italy and the *Taalmerk* in the

Netherlands, for translation companies) and assume that if the company is accredited, the translations will be good. Similarly, many countries have the institution of the *sworn translator*: for a translation to be legally valid, it must be produced (or at least stamped) by a sworn translator, who has passed difficult examinations in order to attain that status (and that stamp!).

ISO-9002 is the member of the ISO 9000 family of international standards that is most applicable to translation, but it is a general quality assurance standard and is not tailored to any particular industry or service sector. It is criticized as expensive to implement – because it entails producing large amounts of documentation to yield an 'audit trail' for all stages in the production process, and then obtaining certification by ISO inspectors – and is unsuited to the small companies and individual suppliers making up the bulk of the translation industry. It encourages a rigid and bureaucratic approach that is no doubt perfect for travel agencies or suppliers of fire extinguishers, but is not ideal for creative processes like translation, where it can be beneficial occasionally to depart from pre-defined procedures (e.g. when innovating or streamlining). Another criticism of ISO-9002 is that it allows each company to define its own quality procedures, which must then be duly documented and inspected. But it does not guarantee that the different companies' standards are comparable with each other.

DIN 2345, on the other hand, was written specifically for the translation industry. The DIN (*Deutsche Industrienorm*) standards enjoy great respect in Germany and elsewhere in Europe (see Commission 1998). The full name of the standard is *DIN 2345 on translation contracts* and it lays down requirements for the source and target texts, the choice of translator, cooperation between the parties to the contract, and procedural matters. It can fairly be said to place unprecedented burdens on the client, for example stating, in point 4.2.3.1: "The client must explain the function of the target text to the translator and identify the target group" and even, in point 4.2.3.2: "The client [...] must not use the translation for any other purpose". Hurray! Client education is all the more likely to succeed if it has the blessing of a DIN standard!

Critics of DIN 2345 point out that it is a self-certification standard, without an external inspection element like ISO; also, that it reflects certain practices in the German translation industry that are not so widespread elsewhere (pricing based on the word count for the target text rather than the source, and no obligation for translators to work exclusively into their mother tongue).

An interesting alternative approach is the *Taalmerk* (language mark) introduced in the Netherlands under the auspices of the Dutch Association of Translation Companies. It is a collective service mark used by companies (not individuals), and it goes beyond DIN 2345 in some respects. These include the following points: it requires double-checking of translations (revision), includes arrangements to settle clients' complaints by an arbitration procedure involving independent specialists, and requires providers to have professional indemnity assurance, which provides a financial guarantee for customers. Finally, it is not a self-certification standard. It requires a thorough inspection before admission and a personal statement every year; once every three years there are random checks among the certified companies.

So we are still looking for the perfect standard – one that works for individuals as well as companies, and that has teeth (strict admission criteria and sanctions in the event of malpractice). Important new standards are in preparation, such as the *ASTM standard* on Language Translation in the US (see Lank 2000). The ASTM (American Society for Testing and Materials) is the largest organization in the world devoted to developing and publishing voluntary standards. It uses a consensus-based approach, involving wide consultation of translation providers and requesters such as LISA (the Localization Industry Standards Association). Interestingly, its first consultation forum for translation requesters, held in association with LISA in September 1999, concluded that quality translation services should be defined as those that adhere to project specifications that are mutually agreed on by the requester and the service provider, instead of attempting to define quality in terms of more subjective, less quantifiable criteria.

AC

The same general line is taken by the proposal made by the Quality Committee of the European Union of Associations of Translation Companies (EUATC), which is an umbrella organization for translation companies throughout Europe. It is working on a new CEN standard for quality procedures in translation companies, not for translation quality as such (CEN = European Committee for Standardization). The EUATC's new standard started life as the draft Quality Standard (QS) and is based on the standards you just mentioned, but also on the EUATC's Code of Conduct and on the Code of Good Practice in Translation drawn up by the European Translation Platform (ETP) (see <http://www2.echo.lu/etp/>).

Here too, the assumption is that if there is a system of accountable and transparent quality control for the translation process, the product will be OK. So the stress is on customer management, resources management, arbitration procedures for 'non-conforming products' (!), sanctions, contracting procedures, etc. (See also Sprung 2000.)

But the proposal seems to have little relevance for individuals or freelance translators. In fact, one general conclusion that we can draw from these industrial standards is simply this: never translate alone! (Would that qualify as the kind of guideline you were looking for earlier?) They all talk about the importance of built-in revision procedures, with other people checking the translator's texts. Any freelance readers of this book might indeed be advised to join up with others, to form mutual co-operation circles, revising and proofreading each others' texts.

EW

Yes, 'Never translate alone!' is an excellent guideline. All in-house translation services and the best translation companies work on that basis.

AC

Another interesting point that emerges from these standards is that not much is said about the qualifications of a good translator. It is simply assumed that since a translation company is working in a business environment it needs to make a profit, so if it employs bad translators it will not survive, because its products will not be competitive. But maybe this is only partly true. Judging by the number of 'non-conforming products' one sees, it seems that questions of product quality do not always play so important a role in competition. Some clients are perhaps more interested in finding someone cheap who can produce something fast. In the field as a whole, there should perhaps be more feedback from consumer to client, and from client to translator.

Or maybe the bad translations are all done by freelance translators? After all, absolutely anyone can set themselves up as a 'professional translator'. When you compare the long accreditation procedure needed to become a professional lawyer or doctor... We need a strong pejorative word to describe a 'quack translator'. Any suggestions?

EW

I can't think of anything better than 'quack translator'. We talk about 'cowboys' too, but that seems unfair on John Wayne et al.

Bad translations are not all done by freelance translators. They sometimes turn out to have been produced by non-translators having a stab at translation because it looks so easy. The whole point of translation standards would be to distinguish between reliable professional translators (including freelances) and the rest.

AC

The EU translation services are perhaps a bit exceptional in this respect, aren't they? Who are you actually competing with, if anyone? If you produce a bad translation, what happens? Nothing? Does someone get the sack, or not get asked to do another one?

EW

As you said, clients are often more interested in finding someone cheap who can produce something fast. If the main concerns are price and speed, the EU's in-house translation services are competing with:

a) freelance translators;
b) translation clients who do their own translations, by whatever means, because they can't wait for us to provide one (we call this 'grey translation');

c) raw machine translation, instantly available to all in-house clients (but not in all language pairs).

Like all in-house services, we are under constant threat of privatization and our political masters are plagued by management consultants extolling the benefits of outsourcing and the wonders of machine translation. We like to think that we already make intelligent use of freelance translators and machine aids. And we also like to think that, given reasonable deadlines, we produce good translations. Outside observers of EU translations (you?) might find things to criticize; but you have no way of telling whether an EU text is a badly-written original, a rushed job, an unrevised freelance translation, a lightly-edited machine translation, a 'grey translation' produced by a non-translator – or, most gallingly, a good translation that has been 'improved' by said non-translator. The process does influence the product, even if applying the right process doesn't guarantee a good product.

What happens if an in-house translator produces a bad translation? Well, first of all, we revise it (and explain why – also known as on-the-job training). If a translator is really incompetent (in which case they are unlikely to pass our entrance examination) it will be spotted in the nine-month trial period and they will not be kept on. If they turn incompetent at a later stage, we would steer them into an alternative job.

What happens if one of our freelance translators produces a bad translation? We try to put it right. We ask for a second opinion. We give them one more chance. Then we strike them off the list of approved contractors.

I sometimes wonder how we manage to mark exams and revise translations with such confidence, when we have no objective way of measuring quality and no agreed standards...

AC

And then another point you raise yourself: the standards are mainly concerned with the process, not the product. Here again there is an underlying assumption: that we all know, don't we, what a good translation is like. So let's just focus on refining the process in order to ensure that our products are closer to this ideal... In the academic field, on the other hand, most of the work on translation quality has been on the product, on how to conceive of this ideal translation. Scholars have tried to open up the assumption that we know what a good translation is like, to problematize it, and sometimes to challenge it. Questions such as the following have been debated at length: who decides about issues of translation quality? What criteria are appropriate to the definition of quality? How can quality be measured? How can translation errors be classified? What kinds of errors are worse than other kinds? Is a bad translation nevertheless still a translation? How can we change people's ideas of what a good translation is like, for instance in the name of higher ethical principles? How can we change the quality assumptions of clients, of consumers, of translators themselves?

These are questions that do not seem to get much attention in industrial standards.

EW

But they are very interesting questions. Have you scholars come up with any answers? If so, I'm sure the devisers of industrial standards would be interested in incorporating them. We saw that the DIN 2345 standard has incorporated the idea that the client must specify the purpose of the translation. The idea of 'agreed project specifications' features in the nascent ASTM standard too.

Don't you think that the declared purpose must be a factor when judging the product? A warts-and-all translation produced 'for information' may provide the information required but may not be fit for publication. A culturally-adapted translation may be fine for selling a product but not for use as evidence in a court case.

AC

Yes, of course. This is part of what is included in the fourth approach I mentioned earlier: that we should know why the translator did what she or he did, and under what conditions, before passing judgement. Your point also has to do with the idea of the *skopos* (aim, goal: mentioned in Chapter 2): we can only assess a translation if we can see it in its context, i.e. if we know what its *skopos* was.

EW

You mention lengthy academic debates on measuring quality and classifying errors. Have they addressed the common misconception that quality is just 'the absence of errors'? When we all know (don't we?) that quality is the presence of something positive, not just the absence of anything negative.

AC

Error analysis, by definition, focusses on errors, so in this sense on negative quality, yes. This is not the whole picture, of course, but it can be a useful procedure, both in translator training and in developing one's self-revision techniques. I'll come to the positive side of product quality assessment in a minute, but let me throw you a couple of ideas from translation error analysis first. (I'll spare you the more excruciating typologies here.)

One distinction that we find useful in teaching is that between language errors and translation errors. A language error has to do with the grammar or style of the translation as a piece of text in its own right, caused by stylistic inconsistency, for instance, or lack of clarity, or ignorance of the correct technical term. A translation error is caused by some methodological fault in the translation process, such as not establishing or maintaining the appropriate equivalence between the two texts, not using the appropriate resources, or not using an optimal translation strategy, breaking a translation norm. We were saying just now that industrial standards focus on the process; in fact their aim seems to be to eliminate precisely these translation errors. After all, anyone working for a respectable translation company presumably already has excellent language skills...

Another useful classification is one between binary errors and non-binary ones (Pym 1992c). A binary error is one that is clearly wrong – obviously the wrong word, or an ungrammatical structure, or the wrong meaning. With these there is no argument. But with non-binary errors there is always room for argument (in the classroom at least!). Binary errors tend to concern language competence; non-binary errors are the stuff of translation competence. A reviser, or a post-editor of a machine-translated text, might wrinkle an eyebrow and prefer an alternative version, but if time is at a premium these might not always be worth bothering about. The time you can invest in correcting non-binary errors also depends of course on the *skopos* of the translation, and how important the translation is.

EW

So 'binary errors' are obvious ones, which have to be put right, and 'non-binary errors' are debatable and don't necessarily need to be corrected... Personally, I think this 'classification' is a bit too facile to be useful. You say you need error analysis for translator training and we all need it for self-revision. Yes, of course. But don't underestimate the other areas in which we practising translators need techniques for error analysis and (even better, if they exist) techniques for objective quality evaluation. We have to mark entrance examinations and use the results to decide which applicants to recruit. Then we have to continue training new recruits where the universities left off. We have to assess the quality of freelance translations and arbitrate between various translation solutions proposed by different parties (a lawyer versus a technical expert versus a plain language fan...). In some of these activities I have found that the translation errors are less important – especially if they can be corrected easily, and won't recur – as long as they are offset by some bright ideas and fresh new solutions. If the quality of an unrevised translation could be mapped on a graph, it would be a series of peaks and troughs, not a flat line. So, to put it crudely, assessing quality is not just a matter of deducting points for errors, but also of adding points for creative solutions.

AC

Agreed. One way of thinking about errors is to see them as deviations from a *norm*. The notion of a norm has been very popular in academic translation studies over the past 20 years or so (see, for example, Bartsch 1987). A norm is traditionally defined as a social notion of correctness.

Norms are *social*: they are shared, in a given community or society; they are agreed. Not necessarily by everyone all the time, but by most people at a particular period, like a consensus. Norms tend to change over time. Within a given society there might even be conflicting norms governing some type of behaviour, until one or another comes to dominate.

Correctness: a norm crystallizes what most people think is the correct way to do something, or what they think is the acceptable standard of a product. A simple example is queuing behaviour, which is strongly determined by norms. There are unspoken rules – norms – about not barging, not going to the front, about how to reserve your place, etc. If you break these norms, you get rude looks or comments, or worse. (The difference between a norm and a convention is that norm-breaking makes you liable to criticism, sanctions; convention-breaking only gives you a reputation for being unconventional. So norms are stronger than conventions.)

Norms thus have a prescriptive force. If you know what a given norm is, and if you accept it, you feel duty-bound to follow it, in the situations where it applies. Norms exert a kind of control. They are constraints on individual freedom, including the freedom of a translator. But they are not laws: norms can be broken, if you are prepared to risk being criticized. And norms do change. Every time you conform to a norm, you strengthen it a bit. Every time you refuse to conform to it, you weaken it a bit.

Some norms are enforced or defined by 'norm authorities' such as parents, teachers, or professional bodies like ISO committees. Others seem to survive simply because people find them useful, they make social life easier.

Norms have long been studied by sociologists, and more recently also by linguists who are interested in the norms of communication. They were brought into translation studies by scholars studying cultural evolution and how this is influenced by translation, usually literary translation (see Schäffner 1999). These scholars have also been interested in the different norms governing (mostly literary) translation in different cultures. Compare France in the 18th century, with its preference for very free adaptations, for example, and the translation tradition in Germany during the Romantic period, where very different norms prevailed. One wonders why such different norms developed, and what happened to them eventually. Such research thus looks at the socio-cultural causes and effects of translations.

EW

Fortunately, we wordface workers don't need to agonize too much over the

causes and effects of our non-literary translations. They have to do with selling products, communicating information, protecting legal rights, enabling
international cooperation (commercial, scientific or political)...

AC

So how do norms relate to our positive quality question? I think norms provide just the concepts we need to understand this.

I think there are four fundamental norms that together define what is meant
by translation quality. I will formulate them here in such a way that they
apply to the translation product, not the process. They thus represent the most
important characteristics of a good translation.

Acceptability norm: appropriate target-language fit
Relation norm: relevant similarity to the source text
Communication norm: optimum intelligibility
Accountability norm: manifest loyalty

1.The *acceptability norm* states that a good translation is one that fits closely
enough into the appropriate family of target-language texts, to which it is
destined to belong. If it fits appropriately, it will meet the readers' expectations about what a translated text (of a given type) should look like, under
given conditions. These expectations depend partly on a reader's normal expectations concerning any kind of text (e.g. grammaticality, text-type
conventions) and partly on expectations concerning texts that are read specifically as translations. Readers may not necessarily be explicitly aware of
these expectations.

Some expectations are qualitative, others quantitative. If you know the
text you are reading is a translation (of a certain kind), you might expect it to
manifest particular stylistic features, for instance. If it does not, maybe this
norm is being broken (which might be a good thing but also might not be).
Quantitative expectations are usually unconscious. We can measure them by
calculating the frequencies of occurrence of various syntactic, lexical and
stylistic features. If we find big differences between the frequency of a feature in non-translated texts and in translations, we can conclude that in this
respect the translations are different from the target-language norm.

Example: In native English texts, the definite article occurs about 7.5 times
every hundred words. If the frequency of the word *the* in translations turns
out to be, say, over 10% of running text, we can say that these translators
seem to be over-using the article and thus breaking the acceptability norm in
this respect. This norm-breaking might be deliberate – maybe the translations
were not supposed to read like originals – but it might be unintended.

2. The *relation norm* governs the relation between the source text and the translation. It says that between the two texts there must be a relation of 'relevant similarity'. The necessary degree and kind of similarity therefore depends on what is relevant – relevant to the purpose of the translation, to the situation in which it has been requested. This is how I would interpret the traditional demand of equivalence. Some texts, after all, need to be translated more closely than others.

The acceptability and relation norms are both intertextual ones. The first constrains the link between the translation and other target-language texts, and the second the link between the translation and the source text. The two remaining norms constrain relationships between people, not texts.

3. The *communication norm* says that the translation should be optimally intelligible, that it should help the original author and/or sender to communicate the appropriate message to the readers. Translators should thus not try to make the reader's job more difficult.

The communication norm has been analyzed in many ways. One classical analysis is that of the American philosopher Paul Grice (1975), who proposed four general pragmatic principles for ideal cooperative communication. These are, roughly speaking: (a) Tell the truth; (b) Say enough, but not too much; (c) Be relevant; and (d) Be clear. If you break these principles, says Grice, you need a good reason, and moreover one that your hearers/readers can understand and accept. Otherwise communication will probably break down.

4. The *accountability norm*, as applied to the translation product, can perhaps be stated most conveniently in a negative form: the translation should not contain any evidence that the translator has been disloyal to any of the parties involved in the communication. This norm is an overtly ethical one. Its relevance may become clearer if we expand the set of parties involved to include not only author, sender, client, and readers but also the translation profession as a whole, whose reputation is at stake. A bad translation – for instance one with many careless errors, or unchecked questions, or uncorrected mistakes simply carried over from a faulty original, or handed in after the deadline – weakens the reputation and status of the whole profession. People begin to think that just about anyone could do a better job than this.

These four general norms give us four positive quality criteria for the translation product: appropriate target-language fit, relevant similarity, optimum intelligibility and manifest loyalty.

EW

I have a few reservations, not so much about the norms themselves, but about the way they relate to the translation product. But I'll come to those later. First of all, the good news: The four theoretical norms can be translated into practical quality control procedures! As an experiment, I tried to relate them to one of the points we mentioned earlier. In Chapter 5, in the extract on Distancing strategies, I quoted a list of at least four features to check in a translation:

> completeness
> accuracy of spelling, numbers and formatting
> clarity of syntax and style
> transmission of the message

and the suggestion that each of these checks could be made into a separate pass through the text, to avoid working on several mental levels at once and so missing some errors.

How do these fit in with the four norms? Maybe something like this? I've added a new feature to check for, marked *.

Acceptability norm – target-language fit
– check for accuracy of spelling and formatting
– check for conventionality* (genre conventions and/or house style)

Relation norm – relevant similarity
– check for accuracy of numbers (Are the dates and figures the same as in the original?)
– check for completeness (Is anything missing? Is all – or all that's needed – reproduced?)

Communication norm – optimum intelligibility
– check for transmission of message
– check for clarity of syntax and style

Accountability norm – manifest loyalty
– the sum of all the above parts??

Now for the reservations. I can't help noticing a few conflicts within and between the four norms. The most obvious problem is with the first: 'The acceptability norm states that a good translation is one that fits closely enough into the appropriate family of target-language texts, to which it is destined to belong. If it fits appropriately, it will meet the readers' expectations about what a translated text (of a given type) should look like...'.

Hold on a minute. What's the translation supposed to look like? A target-language text, or a translation? You seem to be suggesting that a translation is acceptable if it looks like a translation. Are translations 'a family of target-language texts'? Surely not – or if they are, there's something seriously wrong. You even say: 'If you know the text you are reading is a translation (of a certain kind), you might expect it to manifest particular stylistic features...'.

I, on the other hand, would say: if the readers are expecting (or resignedly dreading) a translation that sounds like a translation, it might be nice to surprise them with something that reads like a target-language text – if that is what they need for the purpose in hand (speech, advert, etc.). That's what I mean by positive quality: surpassing the reader's expectations.

The acceptability norm is potentially very useful for judging translation quality, but only if you abandon the idea of translations as a family of texts with specific stylistic features. They must be judged by comparison with texts written in the target language.

In circumstances where the reader's needs and/or specification demand an overt translation (a literal translation of a contract, for legal analysis, or a documentary translation of a degree certificate, for instance), acceptability as a target-language text is not a quality criterion. In such cases it must surely be the second norm, the relation norm, that is paramount. In fact in some quarters, the relation norm is the only one used to judge translation quality, often to the exclusion of the other three norms. This is unfortunate, especially as the concept of relevance is not always taken into account. Of course I agree completely with your statement that: 'The necessary degree and kind of similarity therefore depends on what is relevant – relevant to the purpose of the translation'.

So much for the two intertextual norms. The big problem, for translators, comes with the next one, the communication norm. It would be fine in an ideal world where all original texts are perfect. But what if we're translating an original that breaks the communication norm – too long, unclear, written to impress rather than to communicate? What should the translator do? Produce a translation that's clearer than the original text? No – that would break the relation norm (and perhaps the accountability norm). Produce a translation that meets the relation norm but sounds foreign, so it breaks the acceptability norm as well as the accountability norm (duty to reader and profession)? These are rhetorical questions. I know what to do in practice. But how, in theory, is one supposed to cope when the four norms are incompatible or mutually exclusive?

The accountability norm presents many internal conflicts of its own. We can't be loyal to all these people – 'author, sender, client, and readers but also the translation profession as a whole'. We have to choose. It is a truism that translators have to serve two masters, the author and the reader. Now you've suggested five masters ...

AC

You have doubts about the acceptability norm: remember earlier, when we talked about types of translation, I mentioned the difference between overt translations and covert translations? What the acceptability norm says is that a given translation should meet the expectations that concern this particular translation. It does not say that all translations should be overt, or covert. The point is simply that the degree of 'fit' between the translation and the target language – between the translation and other relevantly related texts – should be whatever it is supposed to be. So a translator needs to know in advance what kind of fit to aim for: one of total naturalness, or some other kind?

Maybe the norm would be better formulated in terms of the same concept of 'relevant similarity' that I used for the relation norm. We could then say that the acceptability norm states that the translation should maintain a relation of relevant similarity to relevantly related texts in the target language... But you might not think this is a very elegant formulation.

EW

No. I'd prefer to say that in order to be acceptable, the translation should look like what it's supposed to be (maintain a resemblance to the intended genre). If it's supposed to look like a translation, then it's fine if it does. If it's supposed to look like something else, it will not be acceptable if it looks like a translation. Example: if you're translating a CV into English for a friend, to help them get a job, the translation should look like an English CV (genre: English CVs – résumés in US English). If you're translating it for the potential employer, to help them judge the applicant's suitability, it is acceptable for the translation to look like a translation (genre: translation). In fact I have no doubts about the acceptability norm, just about the idea of lumping all translations together into a separate class of texts.

AC

Contrary to what you say, I think translations do indeed form a family of target language texts, or rather a group of families, depending on the text type. Scholars nowadays would say that translations form a system within the larger 'polysystem' (or 'system of systems') of a culture's written texts (see Toury 1995; Hermans 1999). This can be shown statistically: there tend to be lots of quantitative differences between translations (of a given text type) and parallel texts (of the same text type), they do have a distinct profile. If you then argue that translations should not in fact be seen as a separate family or textual system, they are not intended to be different – then we are back at the overt/covert distinction again: some are, some aren't. In fact, it's hard to make realistic universal claims about what translations should be like. That's why any attempt at universality – like my norms above – will be pretty abstract, and maybe a bit woolly too.

EW

So why not abandon the attempt at universality, and accept that translations can't all be treated as belonging to a single system, genre or family? Then the norms become a useful way of judging translation quality, as long as one accepts the occasional conflicts between them.

AC

As regards conflicts between norms, this is a genuine problem, I agree. An empirical scholar would be interested to examine the circumstances under which one norm or another tends to take priority, rather than to lay down priorities in advance. Sometimes the reader's interest seems the most important, sometimes the original writer's, sometimes someone else's. I might suggest that the accountability norms take highest precedence, but that would only be a hypothesis, to be tested against the ways translators actually do resolve such conflicts. Are you still expecting the theory to tell you what to do? You say you would know what to do in practice, in the conflict you describe, in the context in which you work. This interests me: what would you do, and why? Whatever it is, I wonder how widespread such a solution would be.

EW

What we do in practice ought to depend on the purpose of the document and the reason why it is being translated. I say 'ought to' because I know that not all translators are sufficiently aware of the need to offer a differentiated service, and they may not have the freedom or the confidence to do so. That's why we need professional guidelines and codes of conduct or, failing that, awareness-raising articles and books (like this one?). All I can talk about is what I do in practice, in one department of the European Commission, where I am responsible for 200 translators working into 11 languages. The 'solutions' that I shall describe here are decisions that have to be taken by translation coordinators or project managers, and then passed on to individual translators. In this particular organization, our responses are conditioned by the fact that we are an in-house service and we serve our institution, and the public, rather than unquestioningly serving 'the client'. If we were a freelance agency intent on maximizing our profits, we would react differently.

Problem: long, unclear originals that break the communication norm.
It is quite common for us to receive a request like this: a 200-page report, written in poor English, to be translated into 10 languages. That is 2000 pages of translation that no freelance agency would refuse: they are paid by the page. But we react differently.
Our solution: change the original. We would say, politely: 'This report is badly written and too long. But it is important, so we suggest that you let us correct the English and shorten it to 150 pages. We don't think you need it all translated into all languages. We suggest complete translation into French and German only; for the other languages, maybe just a translation of the

20-page executive summary will do?' If the client agrees to this (and increasingly, they do) the bottom line will be:

Instead of producing 2000 pages of translation as requested, we edit 200 pages down to 150, translate that into two languages (= 300 pages) and translate the 20 page summary into the eight other languages (= 160 pages). That makes 200 pages of editing and 460 pages of translation, instead of the 2000 pages requested.

How widespread is this type of solution? I can't speak for other organizations, but I imagine it would be quite widespread in services that care about the quality of their output, and have limited resources – especially if the European taxpayer is looking over their shoulder.

AC

I suspect this is not widespread at all, actually, mainly because most translators are paid by the length of the text... But also because few translators have the status (or guts) thus to negotiate with important clients. Good for you! If the EU translation services are not to drown in the next wave of accessions, this kind of solution will surely have to become more generally accepted, or else writers will simply have to be more concise.

EW

Yes, agreed. Now for the next problem: conflicting loyalties and the accountability norm.

This problem is well illustrated by an interesting project we were asked to undertake recently: translating the *Devise pour l' Europe* (Motto for Europe – http://www.motto-europe.org). This was a competition organized by the French newspaper *Ouest-France*; secondary school classes throughout Europe were invited to submit a European motto. The 10 best mottoes per country – 150 in all – were sent to us for translation into all the eleven official languages, so that a shortlist could be produced by an international panel of journalists. The end result was to be a single motto for Europe: something along the lines of: 'United for peace and democracy', ' Our differences are our strength', etc. It would have to work in all 11 official languages plus Latin. Translation was needed to enable the judges to understand the entries submitted, and also to disguise the national origin of each entry. The organizers did not want the judges to know which country the mottoes had come from – they were to be judged on content, not nationality.

When we translated the 150 best mottoes, we came up against a number of loyalty problems. Firstly, it was a competition, so the translations had to be 'fair' – not an improvement on the original entries. I would interpret this as a duty of loyalty to the client: the organizers of the competition.

At the same time, we had to be loyal to the authors – the schoolchildren who had submitted the original mottoes. We must not do them a disservice by producing pedestrian translations of their efforts. We had to ensure 'linguistic equality' – that mottoes written in lesser-known languages such as Greek and Finnish had as good a chance of winning as those in the widely-known languages like French and English.

Naturally we also had to be loyal to the readers: to ensure that the translated mottoes would be effective in their own right and would convey a message without sounding foreign.

It became clear that we would also have to explain objectively why some entries were untranslatable. This I saw as a matter of loyalty to the translation profession: I had to find ways of explaining untranslatability to a lay audience made up of the competition organizers and Eurosceptic journalists who would be only too happy to pick holes in our translations.

The untranslatable mottoes included acrostics (where the initials make up a word) like this one submitted by schoolchildren in the United Kingdom:

> *Equality*
> *Unity*
> *Reform*
> *Opportunity*
> *Peace*
> *Europe.*

It would not be impossible to invent an equivalent motto in all languages, but it would be re-invention, not translation. For example, here is a French translation (close to original):

> *Egalité*
> *Unité*
> *Réforme*
> *Ouverture*
> *Paix*
> *Europe*

German translation (less exact):

> *Einheit*
> *Umwelt*
> *Reform*
> *Optimismus*
> *Partnerschaft*
> *Achtung*

The German version is a re-invention, not a translation. It introduces *Umwelt* (environment) and *Achtung* (respect) which do not feature in the original English motto, and has *Partnerschaft* (partnership) instead of 'peace'. The word for 'peace' in several Germanic languages begins with an 'F' (Danish and Swedish: *fred*; German: *Frieden*) but there is no 'F' in 'Europa', so this important concept has to be omitted, as does 'equality' (*Gleichheit* in German).

Then there were some mottoes that were untranslatable because they had been submitted in (sort of) English:

Original (from Austria): *YOUrope*
Original (from Holland): *Europe = You are up*

There were also plays on existing catchphrases that could be translated perfectly well into some languages but not into all of them:

Original (from Spain): *Haz Europa y no la Guerra*
English translation: *Make Europe not war* (allusion to 'Make love not war')
French translation: *Faites l'Europe, pas la guerre*

This translates well into the Romance languages, but not into the Nordic and Germanic languages because they do not have a single verb like *make* that applies to Europe, love and war.

Rhymes were quite a challenge, and could not always be reproduced in all languages:

Original (from the Netherlands): *Europa is trots, het staat als een rots*
English translation (literal – rhyme not possible): *Europe is proud, it stands like a rock*
French translation (exact equivalent, reproduces rhyme): *L' Europe est fière, solide comme la pierre*

Problems arose with unsuitable content: some mottoes referred to the new millennium (not the theme of the competition), while others contained factual mistakes such as references to fifteen stars on the European flag (there are twelve), or had undesirable political connotations, as in the following example:

Original (from Austria): *AEIOU: Alle Europäer in Optimaler Union* (All Europeans In Optimal Union). This is an attempted overhaul of the old Habsburg motto *Austriae Est Imperare Orbi Universale* (Austria should rule the whole world) and arguably unwise in this context.

We had several weeks to prepare for the project, so like all dutiful project coordinators I tried to find out about recommended methods for translating slogans and mottoes. No theories, guidelines or 'body of knowledge' appeared to exist. Once we had started the job, however, some of the translators suggested that one useful theoretical concept that we could use was Christiane Nord's distinction between **documentary** and **instrumental** translation (see Chapter 4), where documentary translation 'shows what the original says' and instrumental translation 'does what the original tries to do'. To help untangle some of the loyalty conflicts I have described, and face up to the untranslatability problems, we devised a simple solution. We divided the original mottoes into two classes, D and A (we didn't have a class B or C):

Class D – defective motto – untranslatable or unsuitable – *documentary* translation will do;
Class A – viable motto, worth making the effort of *instrumental* translation (recreating a rhyme, for example).

So the first step was to analyze and classify the mottoes. Then we had to ensure that all the 70 translators involved in the project had understood and would follow the Class A / Class D strategy in the same way. On the whole, they did, somewhat to my surprise. It seemed more efficient to channel their creative talents into translating the viable mottoes, rather than trying to turn dross into gold. Also to my surprise, the organizers of the competition agreed to this approach, and were grateful for our input on the relative merits of the competition entries. They even sent a TV crew to film us discussing the mottoes (visibility at last!) and invited me to act as consultant to the competition judges, explaining the translation problems we had encountered and the viability of the mottoes in all languages. One particular problem I encountered, as mentioned above, was that of demonstrating untranslatability and explaining the documentary / instrumental approach to the competition judges. It would have been pointless to use those words, because they are not generally understood – instrumental sounds as if violins should be involved somewhere. **Overt/covert** would not be applicable either. **Overt** might have its uses, but **covert** translation sounds so underhand. So when I was speaking to the 'Motto for Europe' judges, I compromised by talking about **fairly literal** translations of the defective mottoes, and **creative** translations of the viable ones. Here again, some theoretical reinforcement would have been very useful – some agreed principles to which I could have appealed, to justify our methods, and recognized terminology to use when talking about them.

But they don't seem to exist, unfortunately. The terms I suggest in Chapter 4 (straight and naturalized translation) would certainly have come in useful if we had devised them in time for the Motto for Europe competition!

So what do you make of all this? Maybe you'd like to know which motto won? But first, what about the ethical problems – was this a 'good' method? We felt that this differentiated approach allowed us to be loyal to the authors of the mottoes (there is no dishonour in failing to win because your motto is untranslatable), to the readers, to the competition organizers and judges, and to our profession. But perhaps you scholars would say that we translators are exceeding our brief when we start deciding on the quality and viability of the originals we've been given to translate...?

AC

A fascinating example! About possible strategies offered by theoretical research: well, quite a bit has been done on ways of translating wordplay, puns and the like (see Delabastita 1996); also on the different strategies available for translating poetry (see Lefevere 1975; de Beaugrande 1978; Holmes 1988).

But your own solution seems to have served you pretty well.

I find it significant that you found it necessary to interpret a theoretical distinction in terms that your client could more readily understand, terms that were freer of unwanted undertones. Your earlier plea for a more transparent and usable terminology is an important one.

No, I don't think scholars would suggest you were exceeding your brief. On the contrary: they would praise your conscientiousness, your analytical approach, and above all your transparency. All these attributes help to enhance the translator's visibility as a responsible professional. In other words, they add to the translator's trustworthiness.

I take *trust* to be a central ethical value for translators – indeed, for any professional. Without trust, there is no cooperation and society collapses. I think trust is the value that underlies the accountability norm: we have this norm because we share the value of trust. Another ethical value that translators seem to share is truth. This implies that translators should seek to represent the original text or the original author (or, some would say, the cultural Other) in a truthful way, not falsifying the message or intention. (There is more than one way to represent something truthfully, of course.) Then there is the value of clarity, without which communication does not lead to adequate understanding. Anthony Pym (1997) prioritizes the value of cooperation.

There are wider ethical issues, too, having to do with ideological positions. Take feminism, for instance. A feminist translator would be interested in textual strategies like the following:

* How to translate gender-neutral generic pronouns into languages that lack a neutral form? Does the translator automatically write *he* in English, or *he/she* or *s/he* or *she* or *he or she* or *they* or...?

* How to represent speech in such a way that neutral expressions become indicative of gender stereotypes, or not? For instance, at one point in the Old Testament (Genesis 27), the same Hebrew verb meaning *to say* has been translated (by a male translator, into Dutch) in two different ways depending on whether a woman is talking to a man or a man is talking to a woman. The woman *eased [Jacob's] mind* (Dutch: *gerust stellen*) but the man *protested* (Dutch: *protesteren*). In this way, argues the scholar, the translator adds gender-specific colouring to a neutral word and is therefore sexist (see de Vries 1997).

* How to translate some connectors? Sometimes a neutral connector in one language, which might mean *and* or *but*, is translated in a sexist way. Compare: 'I had a female optician, *but* she did a good job' vs. '...*and* she did a good job'.

* How to strengthen the female presence in the text, e.g. by using stronger verbs when the agent is a woman, more expressive adjectives, etc.?

Many of these examples concern decisions about translating a source-text item that is gender-neutral into a language that either forces or allows a gender-specific option. Other cases are more drastic. When the Swedish children's stories about the pirate's daughter Pippi Longstocking (to give Pippi Långstrump her English name) were first translated into French, the translator changed her character quite a bit, making her into a nice little French girl who did not swear so much or contradict her elders or misuse her superhuman strength so blatantly (see Heldner 1993). Some translation scholars – and also the original author, Astrid Lindgren – did not like this solution at all, because it represented an attempt to press Pippi into a more gender-specific role. The translator had used strategies of omission and also made various semantic changes in order to slightly alter Pippi's character, to make her more typically feminine.

EW

In our context – and indeed in any organization – these decisions are not left to the individual translator. If a company has a policy of gender-neutrality, it will expect all its outgoing correspondence and documentation (addressed to the public) to be gender-neutral, otherwise the product might not sell. And this policy will be implemented (via house style) regardless of individual translators' own preferences. Recently I wrote some draft guidelines on this subject and circulated them to my colleagues for comments. One of my suggestions was: 'Don't offend half your readers by using gender-specific language.' A delightful sexist colleague (since retired) returned it annotated with the words 'Instead, irritate the other half by using gender-neutral language'. Many translators are traditionalists, and dislike 'politically correct' formations, but we still have to use them if that's what the job requires. So actually I think this is rather an artificial problem – it's a case where acceptability and house style must take precedence over the translator's personal beliefs.

Gender-neutrality seems to be the norm in most Western European countries, so new solutions have been devised – by authors and academies, not by translators – for languages that have no neutral form. Translators have to learn to recognize these innovations in source texts as well. If you learned German twenty years ago you might think that *StudentInnen* (with a capital 'I' in the middle of the word) is a misprint for *Studentinnen* (female students) but it isn't. It's an alternative way of writing *Student/innen* and means *students (of either sex)*. This device, known as the *Binnen-I* (English: internal-I) is a gender-neutral way of saying *Studenten* (another gender-neutral form is *Studierende*).

It surely has to work the other way round too, if organizations and companies (and therefore their translators) are culturally aware and conscious of their target audience or market. If texts are being translated for use in gender-conscious cultures where language and forms of address are more gender-specific (as in Japan, for example), the translator will have to produce a culturally appropriate translation, even if it is against his or her personal beliefs. Perhaps that's what the French translator of Pippi Longstocking was doing – cultural adaptation?

The idea of rabidly 'promoting a feminist agenda', regardless of acceptability, seems rather unprofessional to me.

AC

Some translators go further still, not in a feminist direction but in other, more political ones. A famous example of an ideologically motivated translation strategy is known as the Cotton Patch Bible, translated by Clarence Jordan in the 1960s. This is a translation that overtly changes the whole setting of the New Testament and places the events in the context of the Black Liberation movement. The global textual strategy is thus 'change the social setting' – a kind of extreme adaptation, governed by a very particular *skopos* that is openly acknowledged by the translator. Here is a brief example from Matthew, chapter 10: the Authorized Version (1611) is on the left and Jordan's translation on the right. The local textual strategies include localization (*black ghetto*), lexical modernizations (*briefing session, God movement, toilet kit...*), cohesion changes (omission of sentence-initial *and*), stylistic shifts (*shebang*) and even place-name changes.

These twelve Jesus sent forth, and commanded them, saying, Go not into the way of the Gentiles, and into [any] city of the Samaritans enter ye not: But go rather to the lost sheep of the house of Israel. And as ye go, preach, saying, The kingdom of heaven is at hand. Heal the sick, cleanse the lepers, raise the dead, cast out devils: freely ye have received, freely give. Provide neither gold, nor silver, nor brass in your purses, Nor scrip for [your] journey, neither two coats, neither shoes, nor yet staves: for the workman is worthy of his meat. And into whatsoever city or town ye shall enter, enquire who in it is worthy; and there abide till ye go thence. And when ye come into an	Jesus held a briefing session and sent out the twelve. 'Don't go after the people of the world,' he said, 'and don't enter the black ghetto. Instead go to the deluded racists of the nation. As you travel, preach on the theme 'THE GOD MOVEMENT IS HERE.' Heal the sick, arouse the sensitive, make the outcasts acceptable, expel devils. Don't bother to take any money or travelers' checks or pocket change, no suitcase, no extra suit, no dress shoes, no toilet kit; for the worker is worth his upkeep. When you go to a city or a town, discover who in it is receptive, and stay there till you're ready to leave. Upon entering a house, introduce yourselves. If the home is receptive, let your

house, salute it. And if the house be worthy, let your peace come upon it: but if it be not worthy, let your peace return to you. And whosoever shall not receive you, nor hear your words, when ye depart out of that house or city, shake off the dust of your feet. Verily I say unto you, It shall be more tolerable for the land of Sodom and Gomorrha in the day of judgement, than for that city.	goodwill and concern rest upon it. If it is not, then hold on to your goodwill and concern. When somebody won't be friendly with you or pay attention to your message, leave that home or city and wash your hands of the whole shebang. I'm telling you a fact, Paris and Berlin will have it easier on the Judgement Day than that city.'

Ring any bells for you?

EW

Well, I think the Black translation is ghastly, but I am not qualified to judge it. I am inordinately attached to the Authorized Version and stopped going to church when the angel started saying *Hi, I have some good news for you* instead of bringing *glad tidings of great joy*. But my views are irrelevant. As we have already said, some (not all) aspects of translation quality can only be judged by the intended target readers. If I were a Black American I might prefer the Cotton Patch Bible. As for ideology and ethics, I would say: the translator who produced it was simply following 'company policy' (which may have coincided with his own political stance) and trying to sell Christianity to a different market. A true professional.

AC

There are also other ethical issues that come up for discussion in the scholarly literature. Some of these we have touched on earlier, like the problem of conflicting loyalties, the translator visibility argument, how to cope with errors in the original, and the best way of representing 'the Other'.

One debate we have not yet mentioned has to do with translator's copyright: this seems to be much stronger in some countries than in others, with very varying interpretations of a concept of *intellectual property*: to what extent do (read: should) translators possess ownership rights to their translations (see Venuti 1995a)?

Another hot topic has been the ethics of the commissioner/client – people have looked at the reasons why certain texts get selected to be translated while other texts are neglected. This mostly has to do with literary translation – for instance, the way in which the West has tended to see the East via translated works which may not have been typical or representative but which were selected in order to reinforce a particular cultural stereotype. At a more detailed level, there has been interesting research on the ethics of omissions and other ideological changes that have been made in 'sensitive' texts. Issues of censorship, for instance – concerning sexual or otherwise taboo ideas (taboo in the target culture, that is). A good example can be found in the early translations of Anne Frank's *Diary*, which manifested some revealing changes in the references to her awakening sexual awareness and attitudes towards Germans (see Lefevere 1992a: ch.5).

Recent theoretical work has stressed the power of translators to manipulate both texts and audiences, and hence their responsibility. I guess it won't be long before we see the first serious attempt to see the translator as a multilingual spin doctor...

Questions have also been raised about a translator's right to refuse to translate a given text, for personal ethical reasons. Would you say this is thoroughly unprofessional?

EW

Not unprofessional exactly, but certainly inconvenient for the client or translation manager. Responsible professionals must think about the consequences of their work, and if translators have strong reservations about translating something, they are entitled to refuse. For example, take a message like *Tell Reggie we've got two kilos of the stuff to hand over outside La Bimba if he brings the dosh*. We might be quite happy to translate this for the police or in a film script, but less keen if it makes us party to a crime. Freelance translators are completely free to turn down jobs they find objectionable. Even in-house translators may indicate their preferences – some of our vegetarian colleagues understandably prefer not to translate graphic and gory slaughterhouse reports. So we give them to non-vegetarians.

You mention translators' copyright. This is not really an issue in a corporate environment where no individual owns any document, translation or original, and there is hardly ever a named author or translator. Although translation is a creative act, it is never truly 'original', in the sense of being fixed and immutable. All translations can be amended or replaced and the body that pays for the translation usually acquires the right to do that. In most translation contracts, the translator surrenders the copyright and other rights to the commissioner, in exchange for the translation fee, in the same way as the author may assign them to the publisher in exchange for royalties. With one difference: translating can be considerably more profitable than writing. Take this book for example. At standard rates, a translator would be paid 8000 euros to translate it, and that fee would be paid regardless of sales. We will have to sell four thousand copies before our combined royalties start to approach that amount.

AC

And of course we're only doing it for the money anyway...

Talking about money and power – what was the winning entry to that competition, who decided, and how?

EW

The winner was *Europe: Unity in diversity*, but no one had actually submitted that motto. It is an interesting case of what I call the 'eclipse of the original', where the translations take over from the original... and then the original has to be changed to match the translations.

This is how it came about:
1. A German-speaking class submitted the motto *Einheit der Vielfalt*.
2. My colleagues translated this into:
    French: *Unité de la diversité*
    English: *Unity in diversity* (because the literal translation, *Unity of diversity,* is meaningless)
    ... and all the other languages.
3. The international panel of journalists that produced the shortlist of seven was not allowed to know the original language because that might create national bias. In effect they discussed everything in English and French. Their discussion went like this: 'The French translation is not correct. It should be *Unité dans la diversité*. Let's put that on the shortlist'.
4. The final jury of VIPs chose *Unity in diversity* as the winning motto, and agreed that the German should be changed to *Einheit in Vielfalt* to bring it into line with the other language versions. They also felt that the word *Europe* should feature. So it became *Europe: Unity in diversity*. In answer to the question 'Who proposed it?' we can say 'Everyone and no one. It is a representative motto and an expression of the common will of Europe's young people'.

At the time of writing, the motto still has the status of a kind offer by the competition organizers, the French newspaper *Ouest France*, and it has not been officially adopted by the EU institutions. Here it is in all the official languages plus Latin and Irish:

ES	Europa: Unidad en la diversidad
DA	Europa: Forenet i mangfoldighed
DE	Europa: Einheit in Vielfalt
EL	Ευρώπη: Διαφορετικοί αλλά ενωμένοι
EN	Europe: Unity in diversity
FR	L'Europe: l'Unité dans la diversité
IT	L'Europa: L'Unità nella diversità
NL	Europa: Eenheid in verscheidenheid
PT	Europa: Unidade na diversidade
FI	Eurooppa: Erilaisina yhdessä
SV	Europa: Förenade i mångfalden
Latin	Europa: In varietate concordia
Irish	Eorpach: Aontacht san Iolracht

7. Help!

AC

Translation is a toolbox skill, says Canadian scholar Candace Séguinot (2000: 95-96). It is not an algorithmic skill based on a single explicit procedure to reach a single correct solution, but a heuristic, problem-solving craft. So you need a good toolbox, containing a good selection of tools. You also need to know how to use these tools, and when to use them.

Some tools are conceptual ones. In Chapter 5 we talked about strategies: these are basic conceptual tools for a professional translator, standard ways of solving frequently recurring problems. We mentioned search strategies for finding information, textual strategies for composing texts, and creative or distancing strategies for getting rid of mental blocks. But there are of course other kinds of tools as well, physical or technical aids. (I suppose the friendly colleague in the next room is also a translation aid, sometimes.)

Simply creating these technical aids is big business nowadays. Journals like *Language International* and the *International Journal for Language and Documentation* are bursting with articles and advertisements proclaiming the merits of the latest computer programs, all aimed at saving the translator's time and energy and the client's money, at boosting quality and productivity, and thus enabling us all to become millionaires.

But has the translator's task really become easier and more productive over the years? Or are we all victims of a gigantic hype? How many translator millionaires do you know?

EW

The technical aids haven't made us millionaires. I don't think that was the intention. The articles and advertisements in the journals may seem irrelevant to many translators, but they serve as useful window-dressing, giving a touch of glamour and a more professional aura to our low-profile craft. My colleague Tim Martin (2000) has written about the image created by:

> [...] specialist journals, where it is not uncommon to find translation companies advertising a whole gamut of services variously described as communications consultancy, documentation management, co-authoring, multilingual text creation and design, etc. A translation element is presumably implicit in all these activities, but the important point is that it alone – however professional its content and presentation – is apparently insufficient to establish a credible corporate image.

So don't knock the glossy journals. In any case, technical aids to translation are not just hype. They have transformed our work over the past few decades. It must be difficult for someone starting work today to imagine what it was like back in the days of typewriters (or worse: pen and paper). When

changing your mind about one word meant re-typing a whole page, or per-
suading a reluctant secretary to do it for you, and then having to proofread
the whole page again, in case new typing errors had been introduced. When
typing pools were noisy places full of clattering typewriters and/or chattering
typists (except on the days when the head of pool had a migraine, so no
noise was permitted, and production ground to a halt). When urgent documents had to be typed directly from dictation onto a wax-coated stencil which
went into a duplicating machine. Stencils could only be corrected with a foul-
smelling liquid like nail varnish (and much reproachful sighing by the typist),
so mistakes were best avoided – it concentrated the mind wonderfully. At
least the dictaphone had been invented when I started work, back in 1972, as
a trainee at the Council of Europe in Strasbourg. How grateful I was to the
audiotypists who taught me how to dictate clearly, by pointing out all my mistakes: telling me to pronounce *the* as 'thee' and *a* as 'ay', otherwise it's
impossible to tell the difference between *with the* and *with a*; instructing me to
use the Americanism *quote/ unquote* instead of the frightfully British *open
inverted commas/ close inverted commas*, lest they fall asleep waiting for
the next word... And for years, when dictation and audiotyping were the
main working method, the typists' mistakes provided us with much innocent
amusement.

For example:

'The Community programme was a muddle of international cooperation.'
(The translator had dictated 'model'.)
'Agricultural products are stored in private whorehouses.'
(The translator had dictated 'warehouses'.)

Now the humour-providing role has been taken over by machine translation.
Who knows what voice recognition will bring? Back to the whorehouses,
maybe?

AC

Voice recognition will perhaps reintroduce something like the earlier divi-
sion of labour – the translator dictates, the machine writes, and then a reviser/
secretary checks. But don't you get the impression that translators are becoming more and more like Lewis Carroll's Red Queen – having to run faster
and faster simply in order to stay in the same place?

EW

Yes. There is a strong feeling among professional translators that computers
can make us waste time. Many of us have to adapt to new software every few
months: freelances do it to keep up with the market and their clients' demands; staff translators have it imposed as in-house policy. Then there is the
other big time-waster: 'fiddling with formatting' – a job that used to be done by

typists, not translators. This subject came up recently in an on-line discussion forum in the European Commission's translation service. One colleague, Bill Grahamslaw, suggested that "we are spending more time on essentially trivial matters of layout and presentation, just because we have the technology to do so". Another, Charles Copeland, put it like this:

> The question is: why are we [...] not producing more? I think I know the answer, but I'm not certain. It is really somewhat paradoxical. For myself, I find that computerization has greatly facilitated my work. Even the most recondite data can now normally be winkled out in a matter of minutes, and searches that would previously have taken the best part of an afternoon can now be accomplished in no time at all. But yet my own experience is not reflected in our overall production figures. How come?
>
> My hypothesis is that many (but by no means all) translators have used computers to dumb themselves down rather than to smart themselves up. In other words, what we are witnessing is yet another example of 'technology biting back'. In the Remington era the division of labour was pretty clear: the translators dictated; the secretary typed up the document. The translator was responsible for the content; the secretary for the presentation. [...] For some strange reason it was considered that this working method should go by the board with the advent of the PC. [...]
>
> The result: the new translator paradigm: the 'workbench' operative, the translator-as-the-operator, a de-skilled jack-of-all-trades who spends most of the day doing work that could be done equally well by a competent secretary at half the cost.

He then goes on to suggest that overall productivity could be increased if translators went back to dictating their translations instead of typing. This is an old-fashioned view – most translators now type their own translations, and have never learned to dictate – but the author is a highly productive translator (a computer enthusiast, but still a determined 'dictator') so he is worth listening to. Some of the most prolific freelance translators also prefer to dictate – and others *might* prefer to, but they can't find a reliable audiotypist. I know one freelance who dictates her translations when feeling alert and best able to concentrate on the non-trivial aspects of 'real translation' – and then audiotypes them herself, later in the day when mental exhaustion strikes. Even in-house, the problem of finding a typist arises sometimes: the moneymen seem to think that secretaries and dictaphones are superfluous once translators have been equipped with their own PCs.

Spending eight hours a day using a keyboard is not good for anyone's health – translator or secretary – because of the obvious risks of repetitive strain injury (RSI) and backache. With a dictaphone, you can translate anywhere: on your exercise bike, in bed, in the garden, on the beach (these options are only open to freelance translators, of course). So dictation skills are probably worth maintaining or developing, not least because another solution is just around the corner, in the new, improved speech recognition software that will allow us to dictate directly to our PCs. Some freelance translators are using the latest products and reporting good results already. Staff translators will not be far behind (software trials and purchases take longer in large organizations). At present only five or six target languages are supported, but this will no doubt change if the software is otherwise viable.

AC

You seem to be surprisingly optimistic about the potential of speech recognition systems. As I hinted above, I can see a risk here that translators' skills may become more and more restricted and specialized, so that a kind of fragmentation takes place in the profession: there will be people who dictate but do not type, secretaries to organize the printouts, revisers who do the checking, and word-processing experts who do the final formatting. Will the translator proper become nothing more than a talking head?

EW

My views about speech recognition software are based on the results already being obtained, not on optimism. The software has improved a lot since the time, about four years ago, when 'Commission of the European Communities' came out as 'remission of the Japanese immunities'.

You seem to think that specialization is dangerous for translators, but that is not the case – specialization is the key to productivity and quality. And there is no risk of fragmentation: if translators dictate, it is not because they cannot type! The standard dictation method is to dictate one's first draft and then to type in one's own corrections and second thoughts when the first draft comes back from the audiotypist.

But many translators dislike dictating. They prefer to type everything themselves, because it gives them more control over the finished product, because they don't have access to an audiotypist, or simply because they don't like the sound of their own voice. Some translators alternate between the two techniques: they type short documents and they use dictation for longer texts or difficult material, where they want to devote their brainpower to real translation problems rather than the mechanics of typing. It is really a matter of choosing the method that suits you best.

AC

I wonder what differences of quality there might be between speaking and writing translators – or even between word-processing and old-fashioned-typing translators. I do not know of any research on this. What about the possible influence of spoken language on a written style? People do not speak the same way as they write.

When you are orally representing something that someone else has written or said, there is already a natural tendency towards a looser, more paraphrastic style. There has been some research showing that interpreters often gravitate towards a less formal style than that of the speeches they are actually interpreting. Translators already tend to use a more standardized style than their originals; an added spoken-to-written dimension might well strengthen this tendency.

EW

It seems a pity if no research has been done on the effect of translation technique (dictation or typing) on translation style. It would be reasonable to assume – but of course this would have to be demonstrated – that dictation produces a more readable result. After all, one of the secrets of effective writing – a piece of advice found in clear writing guides *passim* – is 'If you can easily and comfortably read aloud what you have written, it will read easily from the page. If you can't, re-write it' (or words to that effect).

AC

Hmm, an interesting hypothesis...

EW

Having sung the praises of dictation as a technique, I have to admit that I personally prefer to type my translations myself – on condition that I have an electronic version of the original. I put that up on screen and overtype it. This is a popular way to avoid the problem of recreating complicated formats, because you conserve the format of the original and just concentrate on the words. It works well until you have to deal with the increasingly common phenomenon of texts containing *formatting tags*, such as texts in HTML (hypertext mark-up language). These tags <the bits in pointed brackets like this> can take up more room than the text that needs to be translated, and you will ruin the formatting if you accidentally overtype part of the tag.

Here's an example of a text with tags. See how difficult it is to sift the text to be translated out of the haystack of tags:

```
<BODY><B>
<P align=center>Descriptions des postes au sein de la
direction "Traduction"</P>
<OL>
<P align=justify>
<LI>traducteur adjoint, traducteur, traducteur princi-
pal et réviseur
<P></P>
<OL>
<P align=justify>
<LI>Objectif général
<P></P></B>
<P align=justify>Pour les LA affectés aux "unités
traduisantes", l'objectif
global à atteindre peut se résumer comme suit: </P><B><I>
<P align=justify>Traduire des textes et assurer la qualité
des traductions
```

```
dans le cadre de la mission du service, qui consiste à
répondre de manière
optimale aux besoins et obligations de l'institution
découlant du règlement
no 1/58 du Conseil et de l'article 21 du Traité (CE).
</P></I>
<P align=justify></P>
```

and here's the same text in Word format:

Descriptions des postes au sein de la direction "Traduction"
traducteur adjoint, traducteur, traducteur principal et réviseur

1.1. Objectif général

Pour les LA affectés aux "unités traduisantes", l'objectif global à atteindre peut se résumer comme suit:

Traduire des textes et assurer la qualité des traductions dans le cadre de la mission du service, qui consiste à répondre de manière optimale aux besoins et obligations de l'institution découlant du règlement no 1/58 du Conseil et de l'article 21 du Traité (CE).

There are ways of protecting tags from overwriting, and special software designed for editing HTML texts, but that is yet another product to be installed and learned, when what we want to concentrate on is not formatting, but translation.

Because of the proliferation of new formats, and the problems they present, some ultra-efficient localization companies have systems that strip out the format and allow translators to work on straight text using their favourite word-processing software. We call this the 'cloakroom' system (it sounds better in French: *vestiaire*). When it arrives, the formatted text is 'undressed', translated, and then dressed up again in its original format before being delivered to the client.

AC

Undressed and dressed again presumably by someone else, not the actual translator?

EW

It could be either – or the computer could do the stripping and re-formatting – but if the aim is to increase productivity, and to allow translators to concentrate on what they do best, it makes sense to let a layout expert deal with the formatting. We don't work this way yet in my organization, but I understand that some more profit-oriented translation companies do.

AC

What about research? Will there be someone else to do that? Or do you think this will remain something that the translator proper has to do?

EW

Translators usually do their own research, and I doubt if that will change. We do have documentalists, yes: but their role is to keep the library tidy and well stocked, not to track down the arcane pieces of information translators need. And recently, to dust the library – hardly anyone goes there any more, now we have the Internet. In fact our documentalists and librarians have taken to the Internet too, and spend time adding useful links and maintaining websites. But specific searches are done by the translators, seeking out the exact chunk of information they need to help understand the original, to find the right style and terminology for the target text, etc.

We have already said some things in Chapter 5 about the dwindling role of bilingual dictionaries and the way they have been eclipsed by on-line glossaries and term banks, which contain more abstruse and up-to-date information. Large multilingual term banks like Eurodicautom have existed for several decades and are now universally available thanks to the Internet. But just as paper dictionaries gave way to on-line glossaries, glossaries and term banks are now giving way to full text searching, which allows translators to find terms in a context. As Steve Dyson, a technical translator and communicator, writes in his Internet article 'Terminology Mining' (2000):

> Lexicographers, terminologists, translators and interpreters, to name but a few types of language professionals, agree on the importance of tracking down terms, usage examples, collocations, definitions and more in authentic language contexts (i.e. in documents written directly by mother-tongue authors without second-language constraints or considerations). The Internet is the most powerful resource ever for doing precisely this. Indeed, it is many orders of magnitudes more efficient and cost-effective than, say, ten reserved seats in the world's biggest libraries and ten pairs of eyes scanning all day long in search of solutions to your language problems.

The rest of Steve Dyson's article explains how to create a personal search engine, use metasearch engines and wordbots, compile your own on-line encyclopedia and download complete dictionaries and glossaries. Translators who find all this a bit daunting might like to start by reading another excellent article on the website of the interpreters' association AIIC (Association Internationale des Interprètes de Conférence), in their on-line journal *Communicate!* . This is Andrew Dawrant's 'Using the Web for Conference Preparation' (2000) – the first in a series of articles written for interpreters, but just as useful for translators. It assumes only basic knowledge of the Internet and explains simply and clearly how to use search engines.

AC

So, what about machine translation proper? In my introductory course on translation theory I show students some examples of quite good machine translations (e.g. by Systran), and their comments afterwards are a mixture of shock and horror. They write: can machines really be that good? Are we all wasting our time training to be human translators? Is our only hope to specialize as literary translators, since literature is surely beyond a machine's capability? But how do we make a living then?

The examples I show are not a lot different from translations done by non-professional translators working into a non-native language. (In many countries, the old argument that translators should translate only into their native language is not realistic: there simply aren't enough people around with the necessary bilingual skills.) Compare the progress of machine translation with that of chess-playing computers: a couple of decades ago, I could sometimes beat my computer at chess. Now, a program has defeated the world champion. Will we see the same progress in machine translation, do you think? Progress from the current 'amateur non-native quality' to 'professional non-native' to 'professional native'? How does the machine translation project look from where you sit at the wordface? Will all your work be done by Systran one day?

EW

Let's talk figures before we start on the quality of machine translation (MT). Here at the European Commission, we've been developing and using Systran since 1976. It is now freely and instantly available to all members of staff (translators and people needing translations). But translators have not become extinct; on the contrary, there are more of us. And demand for human translation has not dwindled; it has increased.

At present Systran translates the following language pairs:

Source languages > Target languages:

English	> French, German, Dutch, Spanish, Portuguese, Italian, Greek (test)
French	> English, German, Dutch, Spanish, Portuguese, Italian
German	> English and French
Spanish	> English and French
Greek (test)	> French

If Systran helped us to translate faster, one would expect that translators who can use Systran would have higher productivity levels than those who can't (the Danish, Finnish and Swedish translators). But they don't, and the Danes, Finns and Swedes aren't working longer hours than the others either. There is no evidence of a Systran productivity bonus. I don't want to suggest that Systran isn't being used: it is. Some translators may enjoy using Systran for other, unrelated reasons. Some end users may find that machine translation serves a purpose as a drafting aid, or for information scanning, as an alternative to full human translation. However, as the bean-counters would say, the bottom line is zero gain.

So your students' fears are unfounded. Human translation does seem to have a future. As for judging the quality of machine translation: in the decades we've been dealing with this, a lot has been written – by theorists too no doubt – but there seem to be three simple rules:

Rule 1. You cannot have a valid opinion about a machine translation into a language that is not your mother tongue.
Rule 2. Detached observers have no right to an opinion either – you must really need the translation, or you can't assess its quality.
Rule 3. It helps if you also understand the source language.

So with all due respect, your students – who are presumably native speakers of Finnish, a language not covered by Systran – are disqualified under Rule 1. Sorry about that.

Of course, Systran looks impressive. Your students would be even more impressed if they could see just how fast it is. But it's virtual translation, not the real thing. And surely, without a reliable theory of meaning (...over to you...) it can never be the real thing. Language isn't like chess. Chess rules are complex, but regular, and thousands of possible moves can be tested and compared as long as you have enough computer processing power. Language is a human product and the rules are constantly re-inventing themselves. That is why – contrary to what you suggest – machine translation quality is not currently 'comparable with amateur non-native quality'. Sometimes it is much better than amateur non-native quality and sometimes it is worse. Human quality may be defective, but it will at least be fairly uniform. MT quality is not uniform; it is variable, even within the same language pair, and even within the same text. Therefore it all needs to be laboriously checked and corrected. The checking can take as long as translating the text from scratch. That's why it is not necessarily useful for translators.

AC

I'm not too sure about your Rule 1... but Rule 2 is important: yes, translation quality must be assessed against real need. And yes, machine translation quality of course varies: my illustrations in class were at the top of the range.

You say that machine translation is not necessarily useful for translators – but of course it isn't really for them in the first place, but for people who want translations. More precisely, people who need a given translation quality (say, 'intelligible') in a given time (very fast). Actual machine translation programs are aids for clients rather than wordface workers. If you at the EU are making some use of Systran, it is presumably because the requesters find that it sometimes saves time and money. The bonus is for them, not for the translators themselves.

EW

My Rule 1 – 'You cannot have a valid opinion about a machine translation into a language that is not your mother tongue' – is based on bitter experience. Yes, of course MT is useful in certain language pairs for information scanning – I'll come back to that later. But it is risky, and could even damage your professional reputation, if you assume that it works well into a language you don't understand. To illustrate this point, here's another cautionary tale from Chris Durban's 'Onionskin' column in a recent *ITI Bulletin* (2000):

> A recent case of misapplied MT is visible at Cheesecake World [cheesecake.northwest.com], a down-home site promising gourmets twelve luscious cheesecake recipes by return email from Phoenix, Arizona for a bargain-basement $3.00.
>
> When company president Jeff Johnson stumbled on search engine AltaVista's free on-line translation service Babelfish, he jumped at the chance for worldwide exposure. A few clicks later the site was available in five languages: Spanish, German, French, Italian and Portuguese.
>
> 'It was free: I thought 'why not?" Johnson told the Onionskin.
>
> The results are delectable in their own way. 'Super easy to make! Low in fat, High in taste!' becomes 'Supereinfaches zu bilden! Tief im Fett, stark im Geschmack!' for German gourmets (roughly 'Supereasy things to form! Deep in fat, strong in taste!'). French speakers are offered 'gâteaux au fromage effrayants', literally frightening or spine-chilling cheesecakes (original English: chilled). A sample recipe posted on the site seems unlikely to generate much business from abroad. Quantities are skewed to the point of incomprehensibility, while instructions leave even professionals bemused. Pastry chef Claude Petit, who works at the trendy Man-Ray restaurant near the Champs-Elysées in Paris, was puzzled by the French version, which calls for cakes to be baked until business corporation in the middle ('jusqu'à société au milieu/bis Unternehmen in der Mitte'). He eventually worked it out ('firm'), yet drew the line at stirring in chocolate 'puces' (fleas or computer chips) and applying the chandelier/polish ('administrer le lustre'). In the end, Petit admitted defeat. 'This is ridiculous; the quantities are all wrong and the ingredients make no sense', he complained, noting 'We do not make cakes like this in France'.
>
> But since the recipes are sold in English only, what was the point?
>
> Mr Johnson, who marvels at the Internet's global range, confirmed that his sole aim was to reach out to the world. In this respect, the multilingual initiative has been a success – of sorts. The site gets about 8000 hits a month, and since December, when the foreign language versions went up, he has received an email or two every week criticizing them. 'Today it was a woman in Brazil', he told the Onionskin matter-of-factly'. She said the Portuguese was dreadful; there wasn't a single correct sentence in it.' In contrast, overseas orders have been few and far between: 'We had one once from Puerto Rico'.
>
> Until the Onionskin phoned, it had not crossed Mr Johnson's mind that the

texts might be considered insulting by non-English speakers, and to his credit he seemed genuinely contrite at the thought.

For businesses like Cheesecake World – a one-person company with limited sales and a tiny advertising budget, yet interested in tapping foreign markets – the solution might be to scale down the length of translated text. A short summary paragraph by a professional translator in each language wouldn't break the bank, and would serve up an infinitely more digestible product.

AC

Yes, everyone knows how easy it is to find examples of bad machine translation – like those examples of bad 'tourist English' that circulate on the Net.

> *If you wish breakfast, lift the telephone and our waitress will arrive. This will be enough to bring up your food*

> *We sorry to advise you that by a electric disperfect in the generator master of the elevator we have the necessity that don't give service at our distinguishable guests*

> *Tea in a bag, just like mother*

and so on. These are fun, and usually intelligible despite the mistakes. But are they really representative?

EW

Please re-read the last paragraph about Cheesecake World. There is a serious point being made.

AC

OK, automatic translations of recipes maybe do not work so well, unless the system has been appropriately programmed with the necessary vocabulary, set expressions, etc. Nevertheless, despite the occasional funny errors, someone has thought that these programs are commercially viable, otherwise they would not be there. Who is making the profit? The AltaVista program is a lot less sophisticated than the current Systran one, and examples I have seen of Systran-translated EU texts were clearly intelligible. No doubt you can quote some that were less successful...

EW

Of course the programs are commercially viable – wishful thinking sells a lot of products. But after the fanfare and the honeymoon period, how many commercial companies are using MT to such an extent that they would miss it if it were no longer available? Why not ask one of your colleagues or students to research that?

To come back to my Rule 1 – 'You cannot have a valid opinion about a machine translation into a language that is not your mother tongue'. Even if you have a fairly good knowledge of the target language (unlike poor Mr Johnson in the Cheesecake story), it still holds. Here is an extract from a letter I wrote to our staff magazine in 1988. My aim was to show how non-native speakers of English could commit embarrassing gaffes by assuming that Systran's translations into English were acceptable, when they weren't. Admittedly, the English language is very unfair at times:

> Last year our Systran-assisted output was down to 300 pages – a drop in the ocean of our total workload – but even that yielded a few gems. We had President Delors asking for 'permission to expose himself to the Committee', industrialists 'passing water into the public supply system', and jobless British miners being compensated with '50 books on the Commission Budget' (= *cinquante livres*...). But our all-time favourite is still the classic mistranslation, a few years ago, of the phrase 'les agriculteurs vis-à-vis de la politique agricole commune'. Somehow, Systran managed to translate this as 'farmers live to screw the common agricultural policy'.
>
> Of course, these are only funny if you have a certain knowledge of English [...] You need to know, for example, that 'to expose oneself' means 'to display one's naked body', that 'passing water' means 'urinating', and that 'to screw' means... well, er... 'to extort money'.
>
> Many people working at the Commission do not realize that English and indeed all languages are full of traps of this kind. Many, who once knew, seem to have forgotten. Hence all the chuckling back home over pronouncements in Eurospeak, and the public's growing impression that the Community institutions are out of touch with reality.
>
> If the Commission wants to keep its credibility, it should surely be encouraging its translators to provide a higher-quality service, rather than investing in the cheap and tatty end of the market.

AC

Are you being fair? Even humans can make mistakes. Anyone who asks for a machine translation must know that the results will not be perfect, that there will be a risk. That's why such translations often repeatedly remind readers that they are indeed only raw machine translations, with inserts in the text to this effect.

EW

OK, here are some translations I got out of Systran this morning. They are machine translations of a French article about the Commission's Translation

Service, written by my colleague Josick van Dromme-Desvignes (2000). Here's Systran's English translation:

RAW SYSTRAN TRANSLATION:
The terminological information retrieval
Research almost is necessary for each document, but they depend obviously on its period, on its degree of technicality, of its size, and also of its destination: indeed, as well as all the documents do not have inevitably to be translated into ten languages, similarly, research will less be pushed for a document to classify in a file, while they are probably important for a text intended for the publication.

No embarrassing gaffes, but is that helpful? In case it isn't, here's the French original:

Les recherches documentaire et terminologique

Des recherches sont nécessaires pour presque chaque document, mais elles dépendent évidemment de son délai, de son degré de technicité, de sa taille, et également de sa destination: en effet, de même que tous les documents ne doivent pas forcément être traduits en dix langues, de même, les recherches seront moins poussées pour un document à classer dans un dossier, alors qu'elles seront vraisemblablement importantes pour un texte destiné à la publication.

As I said earlier, MT quality can vary considerably within the same text. To offset the above translation, which I consider to be poor, here is a passage from the same article that came out better, but has a typical sting in the tail:

RAW SYSTRAN TRANSLATION:
To become translator in the Commission
Like any official of the Commission, the translator is recruited within the framework of an <u>open competition</u> which comprises written tests (questions with multiple choice and translation tests into the mother tongue) and an oral test. The translators' competitions cover only one target language at the same time. Certain competitions are inter-institutional, i.e. they are organized to provide posts in several institutions (the Commission, Council, Court of Auditors, according to their needs). Several thousand candidates for about sixty stations are often counted.

Here, again, is the French original. The sting in the tail is the word *postes* (English: 'posts' in this context). Note that Systran translated this correctly in the penultimate sentence ('posts in several institutions'), but wrongly in the last ('sixty stations'). Totally illogical – but then what can one expect? It's brainless.

FRENCH ORIGINAL:

Devenir traducteur à la Commission

Comme tout fonctionnaire de la Commission, le traducteur est recruté dans le cadre d'un <u>concours général</u> qui comporte des épreuves écrites (questions à choix multiple et épreuves de traduction vers la langue maternelle) et une épreuve orale. Les concours de traducteurs portent sur une seule langue cible à la fois. Certains concours sont interinstitutionnels, c'est-à-dire qu'ils sont organisés pour pourvoir des postes dans plusieurs institutions (Commission, Conseil, Cour des comptes, selon leurs besoins). On compte souvent plusieurs milliers de candidats pour une soixantaine de postes.

AC

Well, I understood the gist of the translations OK, they weren't *that* bad. If the gist is what is wanted, where's the quality problem? Cheap and quick...

EW

Quick, yes (but would you want to plough through 40 pages of that stuff, just to get the gist?). Cheap, no. Countless millions have been poured into developing Systran, but let's not go into that now.

This argument brings us back to what we were talking about in Chapters 1 and 2 – 'What is translation?' In Chapter 1 I suggested that there were two extremes: 'Is-it-rat-poison?-translation' and 'Ted-Hughes-translation', and in Chapter 4 we agreed that there are many different products between these two extremes. What always surprises me is that even intelligent people like you are so willing to make concessions over machine translation – impressed by its apparent ability to identify rat poison – and at the same time so critical of the human product, because so few of us come up to the Ted Hughes standard.

So you say you understood the gist of the Systran translations in EW11. Let's define our terms. I suppose you mean that you could see the extracts were about translators rather than penguins, and one of them gave some information about how to get into the Commission, having to pass tests, etc. So that if you were particularly interested in the getting-into-the-Commission bit, you could arrange to have that passage translated properly. Another considerably faster way of getting this information would have been to give the original text to someone who could read it easily, with the words 'What's this about? Does it say anything about how translators are recruited?' Is this what you mean by getting the gist?

AC

Getting the gist can surely mean 'understanding enough to decide whether it is worth requesting a human translation'.

There are two crucial factors that determine the usefulness or otherwise of machine translation (apart from the commercial ones of time and money). The first is what you want the translation for. This obviously influences the kind of quality that would be judged adequate. If you only want to know whether that Vietnamese report mentioned anything about the cause of a particular disease in monkeys, a machine translation might be enough. This might be quicker than waiting for someone else to read the Vietnamese text and report back to you. As we agreed earlier, quality is relative to purpose.

The second factor is the kind of text concerned. It is now well established that machine translation works best for texts with a restricted domain: not general language texts, and certainly not literature, but very specialized ones, where it is much easier to predict the use of vocabulary and grammatical structures (see Melby 1995). The more restricted the domain, the better the system works. Your examples above are not really good ones in this respect – these sorts of texts are not so appropriate for machine translation in the first place. (Exception: the recipe text might have been, if the program had been prepared properly.)

EW

Sorry, but if the European Commission's machine translation system can't translate an article about translation at the Commission, what *can* it translate?

AC

Machine translation works much better with restricted texts like weather forecasts: the Canadian METEO program copes well with English-French translation in this domain, because the range of language needed can be precisely defined. Or the brochures for international mail-order firms, giving brief product descriptions using a limited vocabulary. The Ellos company uses machine translation for its clothes brochures in different languages.

What criteria do you use when deciding whether a text should be translated by Systran or not?

EW

Two other fundamental criteria are the source language and the format of the text to be translated. Taking format first: obviously, the text has to be available in an electronic format that Systran can accept. If texts are on paper only, it's not worth putting them through Systran. Yes, you can type them out or scan them in, but in practice it's quicker to do a human translation in those cases. And although I can almost hear you saying 'surely, everything is in electronic form these days...', I'm afraid it isn't. Think of newspaper articles, which are precisely the type of text we'd like to put through Systran for rapid information scanning, and bear in mind that the web versions (where they exist) are not identical to the printed versions.

The source language is another important criterion. We would make much greater use of Systran if it translated out of the less well-known languages rather than the common ones. But Systran was designed back in the days when computer linguists were still aiming to produce FAHQT (fully-automatic high-quality translation) and to replace translators by machines. A policy decision was therefore taken to develop it in the language pairs that were most heavily used (French into English and English into French) and where the greatest staff savings could be expected. Now, more that twenty-five years on, it has emerged that Systran's main use is not for high-quality translation but for information scanning. But most users in an organization like the European Commission understand English and French well enough to get the gist without the help of machine translation. It is true that some source languages have been added (German and Spanish, and there is an embryonic test version translating Greek into French) but many more would be needed. There are six more official languages which Systran can't translate (Danish, Dutch, Finnish, Italian, Portuguese and Swedish) and at least eleven Eastern European languages (Czech, Hungarian, Polish, etc.) which we will have to cope with in the near future and are already frantically trying to learn.

AC

There is a program developed by the Finnish Kielikone ('Language machine') project that translates from Finnish to English, used e.g. by Nokia for some purposes. But it's not a Systran system. Maybe it could be adapted? Presumably the EU is investing heavily in research to produce machine translation systems that would help with the new languages you mentioned?

EW

The EU institutions have to be careful with the taxpayers' money and spend it only on activities approved by the Member States. Fundamental research into machine translation is not something we can invest in simply for our own needs, although partial finance can be provided for national non-commercial research projects under certain conditions. In view of the unspectacular results obtained with Systran (as far as productivity is concerned) and the non-results obtained with Eurotra (see below), it seems wiser to wait for the market to develop MT systems. Then we can buy them off the shelf in the same way as we buy any other commercial software, as long as they can be adapted to our needs without intellectual property conflicts. If and when the Kielikone system meets these criteria, we might consider buying it – unless free Finnish-into-English MT becomes available first, from some other source. As regards translation out of Czech, Hungarian, Polish, etc., it is still much cheaper to train human translators than to develop MT systems, and occasionally to use non-native speakers for information-quality translations (which is all the MT systems would provide anyway).

Adding new source languages to Systran is extremely expensive and time consuming. It is much cheaper to add new target languages (hence the situation I have described, where we have four and a half source languages and seven and a half targets). This is because Systran is based on a very simple model of the translation process (for 'very simple' read 'insultingly crude' and you will understand why so many translators object to it). Systran's model is the decoding process (cf. your metaphor of 'translation as transcoding' in Chapter 2) whereby French words are converted into English words and hey presto, you have a translation. Of course, to an outsider, translation looks like that. But to a translator, it doesn't feel like that. All translators know that translation is a process with at least three steps:

Step 1: Understanding the source-language message (what Systran calls 'analysis');

Step 2: Visualizing the abstract non-linguistic sense of the message (what you called 'deverbalization' in Chapter 1);

Step 3: Formulating a target-language message that accurately depicts the sense of the original message (Systran calls this 'synthesis').

Systran has no equivalent to Step 2. It does not deverbalize, but attempts to go straight from analysis to synthesis. Other machine translation systems do allow for a Step 2, or an *interlingua*: an abstract depiction of sense which is language-independent. The interlingua then becomes the core of the MT system, and separate analysis modules and synthesis modules can be plugged into it, so it can be extended to cope with new languages. But Systran's great drawback, in terms of its development potential, is that it has no interlingua and it works strictly in set language pairs: so improvements in the French-into-Spanish pair, for example, do not lead to corresponding improvements in the French-into-English pair. And French-into English will be of little help in developing Hungarian-into-English.

All these drawbacks were acknowledged in the late seventies, leading to the ambitious Eurotra programme for a new machine translation system with an interlingua. After much investment, the Eurotra programme was disbanded in 1992 (see Commission 1994).

AC

Yes, the Eurotra project was generally felt to have failed. Apparently it did not turn out to be so easy at all to construct a neutral interlingua that could be used as a basis for synthesizing target texts in several languages. There were also huge organizational and cooperation problems.

EW

In fact there are some Eurotra spinoff projects that are still running today, outside the European Commission, such as the Lingtech project in Denmark (http://www.lingtech.dk/uk3). But inside the Commission we are, by default, still using Systran. Here's a brief outline of the ways we use it:

* As a translation aid

There are some translators who use Systran as a translation aid for full-quality human translation, especially in the French-into-Spanish pair. About 50% of human translation in this pair makes some use of Systran, but as I've already said, there is no perceptible gain in productivity. It is just the method preferred by the translators concerned.

* Raw translation for information scanning

All staff working for the EU institutions can obtain a machine translation of any text for information scanning; they are encouraged to use raw translations wisely, between consenting adults, and not to publish them or put them on the Internet.

* Raw translation as a drafting aid

A common habit that has emerged – again, an idea no one had thought of in the days when FAHQT was the aim – is to use Systran as a drafting aid. In some departments where the main language is French, administrators who have strong English but shaky French may prefer to write their internal memo in English, whizz it through Systran, and then tidy up the result. They find this faster than laboriously composing it in French in the first place.

* Rapid post-editing

A message is sent with every raw translation telling clients that if the quality is not adequate for their purpose, we can carry out rapid post-editing within a few days. This is a service which offers a compromise between speed and quality, and again the end result is not suitable for publication, but will be considerably better than a raw translation. For organizational reasons, this work is done by freelance post-editors at a rate equivalent to about half the normal rate for freelance translation. Demand is high enough to make it worthwhile to offer the service, but not high enough to make a dent in overall demand for human translation.

* Pre-editing

Extensive pre-editing is problematic because it introduces the same queuing constraints as human translation and slows down the process. But some simple routines can be applied to avoid crass MT errors. For example, running a spelling checker and inserting double inverted commas around proper names. Unless the names are clearly marked by double inverted commas at the pre-editing stage, Systran can and will translate them. The name *M. Lange* in a French text was recently translated as *Mr Wrap a baby in swaddling clothes.* When translating in the other direction, from English into French, the famous head of our interpreting service *Ms Van Hoof* became *Mme Camionnette Sabot.* And though brainless, Systran has an uncommonly wide vocabulary of agricultural terms: my colleague *Timothy Cooper* became *Fléau des prés Tonnelier.* (*Fléau des prés* is a weed, usually called *timothy grass* in English; *tonnelier* is a barrel-maker or cooper).

AC

Errare mechanicum est?

EW

As you said earlier, it is now well established that machine translation works best for texts with a restricted domain. You mentioned weather forecasts and the Canadian METEO program for English-French translation in this domain. Apart from the minor quibble that a translation memory system (see below) would probably work even better for a domain as restricted as weather forecasts, you are of course right. Given the brainlessness of MT, its lack of world-knowledge, dubious context-sensitivity (remember how it translated the French word *postes* as 'posts' and 'stations' in adjacent sentences in my example above?) and its inability to 'learn' from post-editing changes (unlike speech recognition systems that 'learn' from the user's corrections), it naturally works best in a restricted field with fairly predictable vocabulary and syntax.

Here again, our use of EC-Systran in the European Commission reflects that reality. We allow the user to specify the subject field, and certain vocabulary and syntax choices will be made accordingly. For example, if the user specifies that the text is the minutes of a meeting, the French present tense (*M. Delors explique qu'il est fier de pouvoir s'exposer au Comité*) will be translated into an English past tense similar to the reported speech used in English minutes (*Mr Delors explained that he was proud...*).

However, this requirement for a specific domain is rather at odds with the information-scanning role of MT – if you haven't a clue what a text is about, because it's in a language you don't understand, it is difficult if not impossible to specify the domain.

Another related area where MT could potentially work well is with *controlled-language input.* Some companies have experimented with this approach for manuals and lists of parts. The authors were instructed to avoid certain terms and constructions that were known to cause problems for the machine translation system, and to formulate the text in a more acceptable way. We did not think this approach would be culturally acceptable in the EU institutions (many of our texts are written in the Member States – imagine the outcry if we asked people to write in a controlled Euro-language).

AC

Apart from machine translation, what about the wide range of *CAT (computer-aided translation)* tools on offer? OK, we already have word processors, spellcheckers and modems, and could not manage without them. You've mentioned the use made of electronic dictionaries and terminology banks. What about text retrieval systems, translation memory systems and integrated 'suites' that offer several text and terminology management products in a single package. Which of these tools do you find most helpful?

EW

Translators seem to agree that full-text retrieval and translation memory are much more promising translation aids than the old brainless MT systems. Strange as it may seem today, unsophisticated applications like text databases and electronic archives are actually more recent developments than MT systems. Until the late 1980s, computers were better at number-crunching than word-crunching, and computer memory was too expensive to be used for mere text storage. Even then, the first text-storage systems were databases containing only high-importance texts. In the EU institutions, that meant EU legislation, which was stored in the CELEX database containing all language versions of EU Regulations, Directives, Recommendations and so on. At first, the database could only be interrogated by a complicated search language, and you had to know the exact reference of the piece of legislation you were looking for. Even then, you had to print the text out – it could not be pasted into your translation, and it was all in upper case anyway. Despite all these drawbacks, it certainly beat searching through paper versions of the *Official Journal of the European Communities*, which is what we had to do before CELEX. Needless to say, CELEX is not just a translation aid but is also invaluable for lawyers and administrators. Now the user interface has been vastly improved, copy-paste is possible and CELEX is available on the Internet at http:// europa.eu.int/celex/.

Another even more recent application that all translators seem to love is the electronic archive of completed translations and originals. Unfortunately we can't share this tool with our freelance translators because the archives contain some confidential documents. In effect this application replaces the paper archives we used to keep, but it is much easier to search and maintain than the old paper-based systems. It is not a sophisticated translation memory system, but simply an on-line collection of everything we have translated in the past few years, with indexing software and a simple method for alignment between different language versions. So we can search for a French term, say, and then move across to the same sentence in any other language version. Typically, a translator will find five or six alternative renderings, and can select one, or reject them all. The only drawback we are beginning to see is the old 'garbage in – garbage out' problem. Because we keep absolutely everything in there (including freelance translations), the 'hits' are not always reliable. So judgement has to be exercised.

AC

This use of archives would explain why some errors or awkward phrasings tend to recur in document after document, if no one ever questions them. A literary critic would bring in the idea of intertextuality here, and be interested to note how much EU texts make use of previously written EU texts. Texts are built on other texts, there are no primary originals, all we can do is cut and paste, not just when we are translating but in all the ways we use language. All the words and phrases have been used before anyway. Sounds dauntingly postmodern!

EW

Sounds depressingly negative. Why do you assume that re-using past translations will lead to replication of errors? One person's improved consistency is evidently another person's perpetuation of poor models. And the scope for postmodernist angst is even greater with the next arrival on the scene: the *translation memory* (TM). This is a generic term used to cover what are also known as translators' memory and translation management systems, with various trade names such as the Translator's Workbench (TWB, a trademark of Trados GmbH).

AC

The development of these translation memory systems was also part of the attempt to move away from machine-generated text to corpora-based systems that use human-translated texts as their basis. This was a logical development because it obviates many of the idiocies of machine translation and mimics the way human translators work when they are translating certain standardized or repetitive texts containing a lot of recycled material. How do translation memory systems work in practice? What do professional translators think of them?

EW

The translation memory is a database containing bilingually matched segments of text (each sentence from the original text is aligned with its translation). The memory of aligned segments can be built up within a text, as you translate, or you can tap a vast shared memory of previously translated material (your colleagues' translations). If a given sentence has been translated before and stored in the translation memory, it can be retrieved and injected into a new translation, or discarded. With repetitive documents (annual or monthly reports, for example) up to 40% of the 'new' text can be recreated from past versions and offered to the translator in the form of preprocessed translation. Often this is in a multi-coloured version showing text segments in different colours to indicate their status: exact matches may be shown in green, fuzzy matches in red, and new text in the original language, in black.

This facility is not restricted to in-house translators: freelances may also find that they are offered texts including pre-processed material – with a reduction in their fee. Naturally, even the pre-processed segments have to be checked and may need to be adapted (if the new text is written for a different audience, for example). But for translators new to the organization, or tackling a new subject field, the translation memory is a very powerful tool.

Predictably perhaps, translators' attitudes to TM vary. It is not as easy to use as the electronic archive and it is not suitable for all texts: only a minority of them contain recycled material. Here at the European Commission, the TM system is most valued by staff translators who have to translate texts written in-house with a lot of borrowings from earlier texts. Some tedious routine material that might once have been considered for machine translation is now more efficiently handled by translation memory instead; checking and tweaking it can be a thankless chore. This has been rather pithily described by freelance translator Cate Avery (1999) as follows: "TWB processing of trademark registration texts is not translation: it is word processing that requires a knowledge of languages".

Freelance translators seem to be more circumspect about TM systems. Of course they never had access to the dusty archives anyway – someone else had to do all the laborious archive searching and photocopying for them – and they're not too wild about the reduced fee paid for pre-processed texts containing a large percentage of injected pre-translated material. Here's an extract from a recent article by freelance translator Andrew Fenner (2000: 9) – perhaps not a typical view, but an interesting one:

> I have taken a conscious decision recently NOT to install translation management [= translation memory] software. That may sound Luddite, indeed, it may well be, but it is a conscious decision based on the work I do, or want to do, and the kind of life I want to lead. There are enough people with no control over their lives as it is: I don't want to be one of them, and have successfully avoided being so for the last fifteen years.
>
> Technology is never neutral, and translation management software is no exception. TMS is used primarily for boring, repetitive, high-volume work – manuals and the like. If that's what you want to do, fine... That's okay, if you're happy to let other people control your life.
>
> Because, to put it quite simply, once you start being paid 33% for complete matches, 50% for fuzzy matches, and the rest of it, you are as much part of the client's mechanized factory system as if you were on their 'shop floor'. You are no longer a homeworker, you are an outworker. [...] Which is where power politics comes in.
>
> Avoiding power politics was one of the main reasons I became a freelancer. [...]
>
> For the individual translator (e.g. me) who wants to stay individual, there is only one real choice: specialize, and go for the high-quality, high-subjective content, low volume, high price market.

AC

So we are back to power again? Ideology? Imperialism?

EW

A bit of an exaggeration, I think. Every organization has its own terms and conventions and we have to use them regardless of our personal preferences. If Barclays Bank want their customer information to talk about *cash machines* rather than *ATMs* or *cashpoints*, is that power politics? If General Motors say they produce *automobiles* rather than *cars*, is that ideology? If the editor of this book requires me to write *organize* and *analyze* with a 'z' instead of an 's', is that imperialism?

'Staying individual' is a luxury that maybe only freelance translators can afford. Staff translators are members of a team, and for them the advantages of a collective memory – and a clever system that finds previously translated material for you – should be obvious. Here is a contrasting view from one of our most junior translators, Neil Bennett, in an intranet forum of the European Commission Translation Service. It is a reply to the comments about the advantages of dictating that I quoted at the beginning of this chapter:

> The ongoing debate about the merits of dictating translations in the traditional way versus the merits of 'new' translation and computer technologies has so far failed to address the obvious point that we all have different skills, and therefore one person's useful tool is another person's waste of time.
> [...] if you are a new, fairly inexperienced translator, struggling to learn all the standard phrases and keywords that have evolved [...] over the years and give English translations produced here their unique style, any system that prompts you with prior translation units is very valuable indeed.

AC

One of the guidelines we managed to agree on was indeed 'Never translate alone'. Are you now saying that in fact it is becoming increasingly difficult to translate alone, even if you might want to? There seems to be a feeling that too much reliance on translation memories, etc. somehow cuts back the translator's freedom, creativity, subjectivity.

One of the ongoing philosophical arguments in translation theory has to do with determinism and free will. The more we talk about the norms and other causal conditions that influence translators' decisions, the less space seems to be left for free will, and the more machine-like the translator's role becomes. This has led some scholars to stress the translator's subjectivity, power and responsibility, and to work for a theory that places human beings at the centre, rather than texts.

But in this respect, translation is surely like any other human activity. We all have free will up to a point, but not absolutely, for none of us lives and works in a vacuum. History and circumstances impinge on what we think and do. Our freedom of action and decision is always limited by what is possible, what is needed, what is desirable, what we know and feel like, and so on. Here we enter the ethics arena again.

EW

Free will is also the freedom to select, to discard, to question. It is no accident that the translation aids most appreciated by translators are the non-coercive ones that allow them some choices, including the choice not to use the aid at all if they don't find it helpful. In any case, language is not just a means of self-expression, it is a means to an end. Our satisfaction comes from the way we deploy it, working within the constraints and playing the rules off against each other. The constraints of language usage are to us what the rope is to the tightrope walker. Without the tightrope, where would s/he be? Free, but bereft.

It is not 'becoming increasingly difficult to translate alone'. If people want to translate alone, they still can. But it is becoming increasingly easy to work together, and surely we should welcome that. Word processors, electronic mail, the Internet, on-line glossaries and text-recycling tools have blurred the distinction between freelance and staff translators. Soon, staff translators will not have to work on company premises any more: they'll be able to work from home if they prefer. Freelance translators who would like to be members of a team (clearly, not all would) can now have access to nearly all the same translation resources as in-house staff. Sociably minded freelance transla-tors can link up with each other to share work, revise each others' translations, help each other out in emergencies...

For the profession generally, this profession of loners trapped in window-less cells, the Internet revolution offers a panoply of ways to cooperate and become more visible: bulletin boards for terminology queries, newsgroups, on-line problem pages (see, for example, Chris Durban and Eugene Seidel's 'Fire Ant and Worker Bee' at http://www.accurapid.com/journal/13fawb.htm). Staff translators also have company intranets and on-line discussion forums – in fact several of the translators' comments in this chapter were culled from our on-line forum.

Electronic mail gives us access to the authors of our texts and to a wider range of subject experts, to discuss translation problems – and the Internet, where so many of our translations are now 'published', can be used to obtain feedback from our readers. As for machine translation... we may find that, paradoxically, Babelfish generates more interest in what goes on at the hu-man wordface.

AC

I like your stress on choice. The economist Amartya Sen has an interesting way of defining human development as an expansion of freedom. By this he means an expansion of capabilities, i.e. an expansion of the range of things you can do, a range in which you have choices. Development then means choice with a larger content.

Translators work in an area in which their range of choice seems to be expanding fast, and some of these new choices have been provided by com-puters and computer tools. It therefore ought to follow that the new technical aids would be welcomed by translators, but your examples show that this is not always the case. Yes, people are different.

I'd like to mention one more point about computer aids that especially concerns translators working out of their native language into a non-native language. Although many theorists seem to assume that all translation – or all professional translation at least – is done into the native language, this is by no means always the case. In many countries there are simply not enough immigrants or expatriates who have an adequate passive knowledge of the local language in order to be able to translate from it into their mother tongues, and who are otherwise qualified and willing to do this kind of work, so native translators simply have to work in both directions (see Campbell 1998).

The main problem then is producing texts that are near enough to native language quality. Yes, you can use native-speaker revisers, if there are enough of them around. But computer corpora can also come in handy here. If you are translating into, say, English, and English is not your native language, you can use corpora to check grammatical structures, collocations, frequencies of items and structures, the typical style or text type associated with a particular item, the kind of vocabulary and phraseology used in a particular field, technical terms in context, and so on. This kind of information can be invaluable in helping the translator to improve the acceptability of the translation (on the use of CAT tools in translator training, see Kenny 1999).

EW

I've never seen computer corpora in action, but the idea sounds interesting – and not just for non-native speakers. Translators who have lived abroad for years ('gone-native' speakers?) might benefit from this kind of information too.

The translators' criticisms I've quoted in this chapter don't mean that technical aids are unwelcome – just that, as you say, people are different. And, as one of the translators so wisely said: "one person's useful tool is another person's waste of time".

Machine translation has in fact done the translation profession a great service. It has shown users just how bad translation can be, and it has clarified the limits and usefulness of gist translation. We should welcome anything that helps users to differentiate between the different translation products on offer.

Having all these technical aids has helped us in another, less obvious way: it has helped us to define the 'magic ingredient' of translation. It's the thing left over that machines can't do. It has to do with human judgement. In Chapter 1 you talked about conceptual tools (transposition, deverbalization, implicitation, explicitation, etc.) and said that they were 'accessible only to human brains'. To my mind, that shows why non-human translation can never work. Translation means choosing: not just choosing the most appropriate aids, or choosing when to recycle and when to re-invent; but choosing where to place your loyalty, choosing the right register for the intended readers, choosing what to make explicit and what can remain implicit.

Conclusions

EW

In the course of our dialogue we've come up with

1. A few useful guidelines (not many, admittedly):
   'Never translate blind. Ask about the purpose and translate accordingly.'
   'Never translate alone.'
   'Hey, look at all these conceptual tools available – try some of these when you get stuck next time.'

2. Some advice on the value of distancing (NB: theorizing is also a form of distancing!)

3. and one useful motto: *I link therefore I am.*

We have made some suggestions for future research and set some tasks for professional associations and the devisers of translation standards.

But I do now see – you have convinced me – that narrowly prescriptive theory wouldn't work. That is not in fact what we translators want or need to help us solve our undoubted problems. Perhaps what we need instead is a different kind of theory, that we could help to create: practice-oriented theory – a theory rooted in best practice, directed at improved practice, and attentive to practitioners throughout the profession.

AC

I started by arguing that translation theory shared the general aim of any scientific endeavour: to understand something – in our case, the phenomenon of translation. One of the big problems has been the fact the concept of 'translation' is difficult to separate from the concept of 'good translation'. In the past, our data have been 'good translations' in the sense that they were published, i.e. thought to be 'good' at least by the publisher and/or client. Nowadays, as translation activity has expanded so enormously, there is more awareness of the existence of not-so-good translations. I therefore agree that modern translation theory should certainly include the study of best practice.

I don't think this means a radically new kind of theory, although it might mean developing new research methods. Our current theoretical models already focus on the causal conditions and effects of translations, in various ways. Effects include evaluations by critics and other readers, reactions such as 'This is an excellent translation' or 'This is a terrible translation'. Studying translation effects therefore means (among other things) looking at people's notions about what, for them, is a 'good' translation, and trying to formulate general standards based on these notions. Such general standards might be valid for a whole society, or even more widely still. This is part of the study of translation norms: examining shared expectations and/or requirements about translation quality – both in general and with regard to particular text types, etc.

Studying the causes of translation, on the other hand, includes the analysis of the conditions under which good translations (i.e. those that meet the agreed standards) are produced, and also those under which not-so-good translations are produced. We can then (and not just in theory!) apply this knowledge in creating conditions that lead to quality translations, and eliminating conditions that do not.

EW

Yes, and of course theorists or translation studies scholars couldn't possibly conduct best practice research without the help of the profession. Surely there could be much more collective rather than individual research (as I said earlier, 'theory' should not be just one person's brain-child).

For example, at the training stage, there should perhaps be more careful selection of students who have the basic aptitude. Other professions do it – couldn't we? If you want to avoid being too prescriptive, you could try to identify the aptitude required by a large-scale descriptive survey of past students – wouldn't it be interesting to see which of them are actually earning a living as translators? Could this have been predicted? You could also ask past students for feedback on training content – is there anything else they wish they had been taught? Different universities could do the same surveys of past students and collate the results... and of course you (or we) could survey professional translators who never had any university-level translation training. With that sort of input, universities could even devise new post-experience courses for mature students of translation.

AC

Yes, agreed. Some small-scale work of this kind has been done, but much more is needed. (Teachers and trainers, though, need not worry about being prescriptive – they have to be!)

EW

Instead of giving my own worm's-eye view of translation studies and what it should or should not be doing, I would like to quote an expert from that field: Yves Gambier, the president of the European Society for Translation Studies (EST). He has posted this message on the EST website (http://est.utu.fi/):

The bulk of present-day TS research has several common characteristics:

 – it is carried out by isolated scholars;
 – it is part of academic training or of a budding academic career, rather than the sustained activity of a mature researcher;
 – it is reflected in numerous papers of varying length and density which generate the feeling that the TS community is composed of authors rather than readers;
 – it uses a variety of methods developed partly in the course of the research, but often borrowed from other disciplines;
 – it is often repetitive, in the choice of topics, in the type of corpus, and in the type of inferences and conclusions it reaches.

Can we be content with this rather static and repetitive nature of most (not all) TS studies at a time of serious challenges associated with changes in the translation environment ? [...]

The emerging professional identity, the new skills and actions required from translators, surely call for new efforts in describing and explaining translation. In my opinion, research paradigms should evolve accordingly:
 – in the choice of the topics (still very much literary-oriented);
 – in the methods (more empirical studies, more statistical surveys... with the increased help of technology)
 – in the scholars' modus operandi (more networking, more teamwork);
 – in the projects' life-cycle (faster results).
(Gambier 1999)

It seems, then, that some scholars are aware of the problem. This is good news for translators.

One part of Yves Gambier's critique that I'd like to highlight is his wonderfully diplomatic point about "the feeling that the TS community is composed of authors rather than readers". This is indeed the feeling of many translators at the wordface: that the ivory-tower-dwellers give higher priority to publishing their own ideas than to digesting those of others – and that they spend very little time reading what is written by translators at the wordface. That's why I have quoted so many professional translators in this book – in the hope that they will be read.

AC

I share some of Yves Gambier's concern about future developments in translation studies, and I hope that scholars will take up the challenges he mentions. 'Borrowing methods from other disciplines' is not necessarily a bad thing, though. Research on best translation practice, for instance, might learn a lot from similar work done in industry and business administration. And having a variety of research methods is surely a good thing, for a subject as complex as translation.

I think such research will supplement, but not replace, current interests and topics. There will still be scholars interested in the special problems of literary translation, in broad trans-cultural issues, in the philosophical conceptual analysis of translation ethics, and so on, just as there will still be scholars interested in specifically cognitive aspects of the translation process.

Having reached the end of this debate (at least in its present published form), I feel both enlightened and chastened. Yes, scholars do talk too much to each other rather than to a wider audience. Yes, we should spend more time studying real translators in real action. And as I hope this book has shown, a dialogue between scholars and professional translators can shed light on both sides.

References

AIIC (Association Internationale des Interprètes de Conférence) <http://www.aiic.net>.

Arrojo, Rosemary (1998) 'The Revision of the Traditional Gap between Theory and Practice and the Empowerment of Translation in Postmodern Times', *The Translator* 4(1): 25-48.

Avery, Cate (1999) 'Case study: translation of Community trademark lists of goods and Services', *Translating for the European Institutions,* 12 March 1999, Proceedings on CD, London, Write Connection, <http://www.writeconnection.co.uk>.

Baker, Mona (ed) (1998) *Routledge Encyclopedia of Translation Studies,* London: Routledge.

Bartsch, Renate (1987) *Norms of Language,* London: Longman.

Berglund, Lars (1990) 'The search for social significance', *Lebende Sprachen* 35(4): 145-151.

Campbell, Stuart (1998) *Translation into the second language,* London: Longman.

Chesterman, Andrew (1997) *Memes of translation: The spread of ideas in translation theory,* Amsterdam: Benjamins.

------ (1998) 'Causes, translations, effects', *Target* 10(2): 201-230.

------ (2000) 'What constitutes 'progress' in Translation Studies?', in Birgitta Englund Dimitrova (ed), *Översättning och tolkning: Rapport från ASLA's höstsymposium, Stockholm, 5-6 november 1998,* Uppsala: ASLA, 33-49.

CIUTI (Conférence Internationale des Instituts Universitaires de Traducteurs et Interprètes) <http://www-gewi.kfunigraz.ac.at/ciuti/index.html>.

Commission (1994) 'Final evaluation of the results of EUROTRA: a specific programme concerning the preparation of the development of an operational EUROTRA system for machine translation', doc. COM/94/0069. Brussels: EC, 1994, ISBN 9277805854.

------ (1998) *Commission – DIN Seminar on the New DIN 2345 Standard, 30 March 1998, Proceedings,* <http://www.echo.lu/mlis/en/document/cec-din-minutes>.

Cross, Graham (1998) 'Book Reviews', *Bulletin of the Institute of Translation and Interpreting (ITI Bulletin),* Feb. 1998: 27.

Dawrant, Andrew (2000) 'Using the web for conference preparation', <http://www.aiic.net>.

de Beaugrande, Robert (1978) *Factors in a Theory of Poetic Translating,* Assen: van Gorcum.

de Bono, Edward (1977) *Lateral thinking: a textbook of creativity,* Harmondsworth: Penguin.

Delabastita, Dirk (ed) (1996) *The Translator* 2(2), special issue on Wordplay in Translation.

Delisle, Jean and Judith Woodsworth (eds) (1995) *Translators through History,* Amsterdam: Benjamins de Vries, Anneke (1997) 'A matter of life and death: Gender stereotypes in some modern Dutch Bible translations', in Mary Snell-Hornby, Zuzana Jettmarová and Klaus Kaindl (eds), *Translation as Intercultural Communication*, Amsterdam: Benjamins, 313-321.

Durban, Chris (1999) 'The Onionskin', *ITI Bulletin*, April 1999: 30.

------ (2000) 'The Onionskin', *ITI Bulletin*, April 2000: 19.

------ and Eugene Seidel (n.d.) 'Fire Ant and Worker Bee', *Translation Journal, The Bottom Line,* <http://www.accurapid.com/journal/13fawb.htm>.

Dyson, Steve (2000) 'Terminology mining', <http://www.sdc-language.com/term.htm>.

Ellison, Ralph (1952) *The Invisible Man*, New York: Random House.

European Year of Languages 2001, <http://www.eurolang2001.org/> or <http://europa.eu.int/comm/education/languages/actions/year2001.html>.

Fawcett, Peter (1997) *Translation and Language*, Manchester: St. Jerome Publishing.

Fenner, Andrew (2000) 'The Choices Facing Translators', *ITI Bulletin*, April 2000: 9.

FIT (Fédération Internationale des Traducteurs) <http://www.fit-ift.org>

Flotow, Luise von (1997) *Translation and Gender*, Manchester: St. Jerome Publishing.

Fraser, Bill, & Helen Titchen (1998) 'Distancing Strategies', EC Translation Service intranet. Similar material should be available soon in the Workshops for Translators section of <http://europa.eu.int/comm/translation/theory/>.

Gambier, Yves (1999) 'Message from the EST President', *EST Newsletter* 15, December 1999, http://est.utu.fi/.

Gouadec, Daniel (1990) 'Traduction signalétique', *Meta* 35(2): 332-341.

Grice, Paul (1975) 'Logic and conversation', in P. Cole and J.L. Morgan (eds), *Syntax and Semantics, 3: Speech Acts*, New York: Academic Press, 41-58.

Gutt, Ernst-August (2000) *Translation and Relevance. Cognition and Context*, Second Editon, Manchester: St. Jerome Publishing.

Heldner, Christina (1993) 'Une anarchiste en camisole de force. Fifi Brandacier ou la métamorphose française de Pippi Långstrump', *Moderna Språk* 87(1): 37-43.

Hermans, Theo (ed) (1985) *The Manipulation of Literature. Studies in Literary Translation*, London: Croom Helm.

------ (1999) *Translation in Systems*, Manchester: St. Jerome Publishing.

Holmes, James S. (1988) *Translated! Papers on Literary Translation and Translation Studies*, Amsterdam: Rodopi.

Hönig, Hans. G. and Paul Kussmaul (1982) *Strategie der Übersetzung: Ein Lehr- und Arbeitsbuch*, Tübingen: Narr.

House, Juliane (1997) *Translation Quality Assessment: A Model Revisited*, Tübingen: Narr.

ITI (Institute of Translation and Interpreting) <http://www.iti.org.uk>.

Jääskeläinen, Riitta (1998) 'Think-aloud protocols', in M. Baker (ed), 265-269.

Jordan, Clarence (1963-1970) *The Cotton Patch Bible*, Piscataway, NJ: New Century.

Kenny, Dorothy (1999) 'CAT tools in an academic environment: what are they good for?', *Target* 11(1): 65-82.

Koller, Werner (1972) *Grundprobleme der Übersetzungstheorie*, Bern: Francke.

Kussmaul, Paul and Sonja Tirkkonen-Condit (1995) 'Think-aloud protocol analysis in translation studies', *TTR* 8(1): 177-199.

Lank, Steve (2000) 'ASTM Standard for Language Translation', January 2000, *Translation Journal*, <http://accurapid.com/journal/>.

Laviosa-Braithwaite, Sara (1998) 'Universals of translation', in M. Baker (ed), 288-291.

Lefevere, André (1975) *Translating Poetry: Seven Strategies and a Blueprint*, Assen & Amsterdam: van Gorcum.

------ (1992a) *Translation, Rewriting and the Manipulation of Literary Fame*, London: Routledge.

------ (1992b) *Translation/History/Culture*. London: Routledge.

LISA (Localization Industry Standards Association): <http://www.lisa.org>.

Martin, Tim (2000) 'Image and self-image', <http://europa.eu.int/comm/translation/theory/>.

Melby, Alan (1995) *The Possibility of Language*, Amsterdam: Benjamins.

Nairobi Declaration (1976) <http://www.fit-ift.org/english/nairo-e.html>.

Neubert, Albrecht and Gregory M. Shreve (1992) *Translation as Text*, Kent, Ohio: Kent State University Press.

Newmark, Peter (1981) *Approaches to Translation*, Oxford: Pergamon Press.

------ (1988) *A Textbook of Translation*, New York: Prentice Hall.

Nida, Eugene A. (1964) *Toward a Science of Translating*, Leiden: Brill.

------ and Charles R. Taber (1969) *The Theory and Practice of Translation*, Leiden: Brill.

Nord, Christiane (1997) *Translating as a Purposeful Activity*, Manchester: St. Jerome Publishing.

Oittinen, Riitta (1993) *I am Me – I am Other: On the dialogics of translating for children*, Tampere: University of Tampere.

Pym, Anthony (1992a) 'The relation between translation and material text transfer', *Target* 4(2): 171-189.

------ (1992b) *Translation and Text Transfer*, Frankfurt am Main: Lang.

------ (1992c) 'Translation error analysis and the interface with language teaching', in C. Dollerup and A. Loddegaard (eds), *Teaching Translation and Interpreting: Training, Talent and Experience*, Amsterdam: Benjamins, 279-288.

------ (1997) *Pour une éthique du traducteur*, Arras: Artois Presses Université.

Reiss, Katharina (2000) *Translation Criticism: Potential and Limitations*, translated by Erroll F. Rhodes, Manchester: St. Jerome Publishing / American Bible Society (originally published in German in 1971).

------ and Hans J. Vermeer (1984) *Grundlegung einer Allgemeinen Translationstheorie*, Tübingen: Niemeyer.

Robinson, Douglas (1996) *Translation and Taboo*, DeKalb, Ill.: Northern Illinois University Press.

------ (1997a) *Western Translation Theory from Herodotus to Nietzsche*, Manchester: St Jerome Publishing.

------ (1997b) *Translation and Empire*, Manchester: St. Jerome Publishing.

Sager, Juan (1994) *Language Engineering and Translation – Consequences of automation*, Amsterdam & Philadelphia: Benjamins.

Samuelsson-Brown, Geoffrey (1993) *A Practical Guide for Translators*, Clevedon: Multilingual Matters

Schäffner, Christina (ed) (1998), *Translation and Quality*, Clevedon: Multilingual Matters.

------ (1999) *Translation and Norms*, Clevedon: Multilingual Matters.

Séguinot, Candace (2000) 'Knowledge, theory and expertise in translation', in A. Chesterman, N. Gallardo and Y. Gambier (eds), *Translation in Context*, Amsterdam: Benjamins, 87-104.

Shuttleworth, Mark and Moira Cowie (1997) *Dictionary of Translation Studies*, Manchester: St. Jerome Publishing.

Simeoni, Daniel (1998) 'The pivotal status of the translator's habitus', *Target* 10(1): 1-39.

Snell-Hornby, Mary, Hans G. Hönig, Paul Kussmaul and Peter A. Schmitt (eds) (1998) *Handbuch Translation*, Tübingen: Stauffenburg.

Sprung, Robert C. (ed) (2000) *Translating into Success*, Amsterdam: Benjamins.

Stetting, Karen (1989) 'Transediting – a new term for coping with a grey area between editing and translating', in G. Caie *et al.* (eds), *Proceedings from the Fourth Nordic Conference for English Studies*, Copenhagen: Department of English, University of Copenhagen, 371-382.

Tabakowska, Elzbieta (1998) 'Polish tradition', in M. Baker (ed), 523-532.

Thomas, F. and O. Johnson (1981) *Disney animation – the Illusion of Life*, New York: Abbeyville Press.

Toury, Gideon (1995) *Descriptive Translation Studies and Beyond*, Amsterdam & Philadelphia: Benjamins.

TTR (Traduction, Terminologie, Rédaction) (1989) Special issue 2(2) on Error Analysis in translation.

van Dromme-Desvignes, Josick (2000) 'La traduction au service de la construction européenne: le service de traduction de la Commission', *Le Linguiste* (Bulletin trimestriel de la Chambre belge des traducteurs, interprètes et philologues) 46(3): 23-37.

Venuti, Lawrence (1995a) 'Translation, Authorship, Copyright', *The Translator* 1(1): 1-24.

------ (1995b) *The Translator's Invisibility: A History of Translation*, London: Routledge.

Vieira, Else (1994) 'A postmodern translational aesthetics in Brazil', in Mary Snell-Hornby, Franz Pöchhacker and Klaus Kaindl (eds), *Translation Studies: An interdiscipline*, Amsterdam & Philadelphia: Benjamins, 65-72.

Vinay, J-P. and J. Darbelnet (1958) *Stylistique comparée du français et de l'anglais*. Paris: Didier.

Wagner, Emma (1988) 'Les lecteurs écrivent', *Commission Courrier du Person-*

nel (November 1988): 76.
Waterfield, Robin (trans) (1982) Plato: *Philebus*, Harmondsworth: Penguin.
Weaver, William (1955) 'Translation', in W.N. Locke and A.D. Booth (eds), *Machine Translation of Languages*, New York: Wiley, 15-23.
Wilson, E. O. (1998) *Consilience,* London: Little, Brown & Company.

Index

absolute translation, 52
abstract translation, 52
academic writing style, 60, 76
acceptability norm, 92, 94
    definition, 92
accountability norm, 92, 94
    definition, 93
accreditation system, need for, 37
adaptation vs foreignization, 58
advertising and marketing, 45
Aeschylus, 5
AIIC (Association Internationale des Interprètes de Conférence), 35-37, 114, 137
aims of theory, 2, 133
Alberge, Dalya, 27
artistic translation, 53
ASTM standard, 86, 89
audiotyping, 109
author
    dead vs alive, 17
    demotion of, 24
    need to contact, 48
    single vs collective, 25, 28
    vs client, 49
Avery, Cate, 129, 137

Babelfish, 117, 131
background texts, 73, 74
bad vs good translation, 37, 87, 88
Bartsch, Renate, 91, 137
belles infidèles, 16
Bennett, Neil, 130
Berglund, Lars, 1
best practice research, 133-135
Bible translation, 4, 104
binary classifications of translation types, 49
Binnen-I (gender-neutral device), 103
Black Liberation movement, 104

brief, briefing,
    need for translation brief, 39-48, 101-104, 122, 125
    questions to be asked, 47
Bühler, Karl, 46, 47
builder, translator as, 13

carnival (postmodern metaphor), 25
CELEX database, 127
CEN (European Committee for Standardization), 86
censor, translator as, 17, 22
censorship, 106
Chair Theory, 3
Cheesecake World, 117
chess vs language, 116
chess-playing computers, 115
Chinese whispers, 48
choice in translation, 131
chunking, 10
CIUTI (Conférence Internationale des Instituts Universitaires de Traducteurs et Interprètes), 36
client
    clients' priorities, 87
    types of translation client, 49
    vs author, 49
coffee, complexity of ordering, 48
common knowledge, 76
common sense, 48, 65
communication
    client to translator, 42
    pragmatic principles for, 93
    stages of, 43
    translation as, 19
    translator to reader, 42
communication norm, 92, 94
    definition, 93
communicative vs semantic translation, 49, 50